Wired to Self-Destruct

by

James Prest

TEACH Services, Inc.
P U B L I S H I N G
www.TEACHServices.com

_____

Copyright revised © 2011 TEACH Services, Inc.
ISBN-13: 978-1-57258-692-5 (Paperback)
ISBN-13: 978-1-57258-693-2 (Hardback)
ISBN-13: 978-1-57258-694-7- (E-Book)
Library of Congress Control Number: 2011941077

All scripture quotations are taken from the King James Version Bible.

The names in this book are pseudonyms.

Published by

TEACH Services, Inc.

P U B L I S H I N G

www.TEACHServices.com

Dedication

This book is dedicated to Jack.

Acknowledgments

I want to thank my father, Wilton Prest, for showing me a better way. I want to thank my mother, Evelyn Prest, for loving her children oh so much. I want to thank my older sisters, Alicia and Kristin, for helping me to understand myself and thus get me out of the rut I was in. Thanks to my younger brother, Charlie, for being real and not faking everything. Thanks to my little sister, Grace, for caring and being so attentive to me. And thanks to my youngest brother, John, for trying so hard.

These acknowledgments would not be complete without thanking my friends Samantha Gould, Jarla Aviles, Doris Vinales, Amy Beard, Monica Hahn, Beth Johns, Tiffany Miller, Ricky Mackin, and Ace Hedger for simply being there for me and encouraging me to keep going. I love you all! Thanks for everything!

Table of Contents

Chapter 1

Human Rights

"He's right over there. Why don't you help him? Don't just sit there! Look at him! He's sitting on the edge of the street despising his own life. His head is bowed down in sorrow; his spirits are crushed. He's sad and discouraged, and he sees no reason to bother hoping anymore. He's afraid to hope. Why don't you do something?! Don't you understand him?! I don't think he can hear you Jack. Jack, get up off the curb. Jack? Jack, can you hear me?"

Every human being has the right to be treated with respect. Anyone who, for *any* reason, infringes upon this right of another is guilty of theft. There is no person on the entire globe that has the authority to steal away the rights of others. It matters not what excuse or "reason" may be given in justification of stealing away the rights of others, it is stealing, and it is wrong.

Every human being has the right to be treated with respect. Anyone who, for any reason, infringes upon this right of another is guilty of theft.

When the right to be treated with respect is violated, the mind of the one who was intruded upon subconsciously takes action to defend against the intruder. This is a law of human mind that is often carried out in the subconscious. It is a principle inculcated in the defense mechanism of every individual.

This right can be encroached upon in countless ways. But to put it in its simplest form, any word, look, action, occurrence, or non-occurrence that causes another individual to *feel* emotional discomfort is a violation of that individual's right to be treated with respect. It is an encroachment, an infringement of his personal rights. It is an intruder, and the defense systems of all human beings are programmed to defend against it.

If you place your finger on a hot coal, you do not need to think, "Ouch! This hurts! I should remove my finger," and then make a conscious effort to remove your finger from the hot coal. No. It is an automatic, subconscious reaction of the nervous system to pain; it is the same thing with emotional pain. It is not necessary to take a conscious action to divert the emotional pain that one is experiencing. The human mind deals with these things in the subconscious.

> *When the right to be treated with respect is violated, the mind of the one who was intruded upon subconsciously takes action to defend against the intruder.*

This is where one of the grandest problems that have ever affected the human race comes into play. More often than not, the subconscious reaction of the brain to emotional pain is a response that often makes our life more difficult and painful than it needs to be.

For a practical example of this, let us imagine a child who is being corrected by his parent because he did something wrong. The parent violates the child's right to be treated with respect by giving the child an angry look and scolding him roughly with harsh words. The child feels the emotional discomfort and pain as he sees his parent's enraged look and hears the hurtful words. His brain then takes subconscious action to avoid the pain by looking away from what is causing part of his pain—the angry look on his parent's face.

When the child looks away from his parent, the parent becomes more enraged and tells the child to look him in the eyes when he is speaking to him. The child has difficulty doing this, not necessarily because he is a rebellious and obstinate child, but because it causes him emotional pain to behold the scary face of his parent. The child then gets into more trouble for not obeying his parent by looking him in the eyes.

This is a very simple and basic example of how the subconscious takes control of matters and ends up resulting in more pain to the already violated individual.

This principle of the human mind avoiding emotional pain through taking subconscious action to divert it is the grand foundational principle that must be understood by those who seek to benefit others through their influence. It is impossible to gain the fullest trust and respect from others when this principle is not carried out toward those you want to help.

This book is not designed to tell you what to do in every situation, but rather it is designed to give, explain, and illustrate the core principles of the human mind so that no matter what the case is, whether the problem is yours or someone else's, you will have the tools necessary to find out exactly what to do, as far as possible, to fix the problem at hand and alleviate the emotional pain that others are causing you and that you might be causing others, thus deleting the negative effects of such pain.

Pay close attention! This book is not written to be read and then put down so that you can read the next book on your list. The principles in this book need to be studied and applied in your life so that you can be a happier person and be able to share that happiness with others. It is one thing to read a book, it is another thing to understand it, and still another thing to actually use the information to your advantage. Gather all that you can from this book. There is valuable information in it. That's a promise.

Chapter 2

The Rejection Process

Rejection is the term used to represent emotional discomfort. The process of rejection is a very simple and basic concept that is easily understood. When a person suffers emotional discomfort, his brain calculates the information and stores the painful data subconsciously. The file with the painful data is used as an information update to enable the individual to avoid and ward off emotional pain. As more and more emotional discomfort is experienced, the painful data file is updated and continues to gain more and more information.

Rejection Habits

Feelings of rejection experienced in one's life play a large role in developing thoughts in one's mind. These, in turn, bring forth responses or actions that, if continued, soon become habits. Habits in turn make up a large part of one's character, and the character of an individual determines his ability to successfully get along with himself and others. Put simply, it affects every aspect of his life for weal or for woe. For a practical example of how this works, let us examine the life of a child

When a person suffers emotional discomfort, his brain calculates the information and stores the painful data ... to enable the individual to avoid and ward off emotional pain.

through the years.

While growing up, children receive things from their parents all the time. From toys to breakfast foods to clothing, they are constantly receiving things from their parents. This one particular child, however, is always led to feel like he owes his parents the world for everything he receives. The reason that the child feels this way is because his parents are always reminding him of the things they have done for him. They use it as a driving motive of why he ought to be a good child and do what he is told and help out with the chores and so forth.

Through years of experience with his parents, friends, and teachers, the child's mind arrives at the understanding that if someone does something for him he is indebted to them until payment is made. This understanding comes from the painful rejection data that has been updated throughout his entire life.

The condition of being in debt is not a good feeling—it can be very emotionally discomforting, especially if the debt cannot be paid off within a short period of time. As a natural result of this, the brain takes either conscious or subconscious action to avoid the discomfort. In this instance of our featured child, he makes a half-conscious choice to avoid the discomfort by being very cautious about receiving anything from anyone. His caution often proves unsuccessful as, on many occasions, he finds strings attached to the gifts he has hesitatingly chosen to receive. It is the most natural thing in the world for him to choose to never receive any gifts from anyone under any circumstances, and it is very easy to see how this could cause major social problems.

Suppose a girl goes through the rejection process, and it leads her to reject all gifts from anyone because she doesn't want to feel the emotional discomfort of it all. She doesn't want to feel like she is in perpetual debt and then feel guilty because she can't pay it off. To her, it is not worth it. In her mind, it is easier to starve to death then to receive food from someone because it just seems far less painful. Her reasoning is, "Why live in emotional misery when you can die in peace?" And what's wrong with her reasoning? Who wouldn't choose a peaceful death over a living hell?

On becoming of age, she contemplates marriage. Finally, one day her future husband comes to her with a nicely wrapped gift. Now what? Everything she has ever learned and experienced in the past about receiving gifts from people points to the fact that it is not worth it. "Die first" is the law of her life.

Many people would say that in such an extreme situation as this scenario the girl would take the gift and suffer through the emotional distress of feeling indebted if she couldn't get over it, but this is not always true. Rejection can be as strong as death to control its victim— it doesn't have to be that strong, but it can be. Should this girl reject the gift most momentary onlookers would say that she has a problem and they hope the man realizes she is a jerk. They would counsel him to move on and find someone else. But should they understand the behind-the-scenes story of her life, they might have a bit of compassion on her and seek to help her.

Uninformed individuals, know-it-alls, who know nothing of this girl's experience would say that she is a freak and that she would have to be a complete idiot to reject the gift. But stop for one minute and try to enter the mind of this poor girl.

For the past twenty years of her life the painful rejection data has been continually updated with information, proving to her almost beyond repair that all gifts have strings attached. She has been told by her friends and relatives that this is not so, but this is just a theory to her. She's lived her whole life feeling as if she owed everyone the world and that she would never be free from debt. It's a nice theory

12

to her that she could actually receive a free gift, but to her it is *not* practical.

She's been violated since she was a child. Her belief system has been severely marred. Those friends who promised her that there were no strings attached to their gifts, in the moment of temptation, quickly reminded her of all they had done for her and that she, therefore, needed to act a certain way. She has nothing foundational upon which to accept the theory that she can receive a truly free gift. The only foundation she has, which has been so thoroughly engrained in the deepest recesses of her mind, is that solitary file of painful data that *will not allow her* to hurt herself again by accepting another "free" gift. For her to choose to accept a gift would be for her to choose to inflict pain upon herself, and she *will not do it*.

> *There seems to be literally no limit to the possible habits that can develop as a means of defending against emotional pain.*

Call her an idiot, call her a freak, and add to her emotional pain if you will, but this will not help her. It will only confirm in her mind the lie that all love and gifts are conditional, that they always have been, and *always will be*.

Refusing gifts from people because of conscious or subconscious fears that you will have to pay them back is just one type of rejection habit. There seems to be literally no limit to the possible habits that can develop as a means of defending against emotional pain.

The Belief System

If people live through their childhood, youth, and even adult years being emotionally abused, it will become part of their belief system.

The painful rejection data becomes so insisting upon them that they are basically forced to acknowledge the conclusion of the information that the painful file has on record. In other words, it will be to them the only way of life. In their mind they have never really been accepted before, and so they never expect it. Rather, they always expect rejection because that is all they've ever received, and therefore, they act like they will be rejected. This is normal for them, and why should they act like someone they are not? Rejection has become a part of them. Acting like they are and will be rejected is who they are, and they cannot change it. Accept or reject them, but they will act the same.

This is not a problem in and of itself, but it proves itself one of the grandest of all problems to the violated individual when it comes to their social life. When people really do accept them unconditionally, they act like they are being rejected. Do you see how this could very quickly cause some major problems?

The painful rejection data becomes so insisting upon them that they are basically forced to acknowledge the conclusion of the information that the painful file has on record.

To give a quick illustration of how the process of changing the belief system works, picture a little girl whose favorite animal is a dog; however, she has never petted a dog before. Unfortunately, for her, her first attempt proved painful— the dog bit her! She doesn't hate dogs now just because she was bitten by this one. Surely she can pet other dogs without being bitten. She takes advantage of her next opportunity to pet a different dog. She is cautious this time because of the result of her first attempt. Sadly, she is again bitten, but this time harder than the last, bringing her more pain.

And so the girl, in her desire to get closer to her favorite animal, continues to try to pet different dogs, being more and more cautious and careful as she continually gets bitten. Eventually, as you may guess, the girl ceases to attempt to pet dogs anymore because she believes that all dogs will bite her.

Why does she believe this? Her scared hands testify to its truth. She never enjoyed the pain when the dogs bit her, but the hope of intimacy with one motivated her to keep trying. But eventually, the pain and tears with no reward was no longer the desired path. Why suffer for nothing? If the dog was what gave her pain, then the best thing to do to avoid pain would be to stay away from dogs—period. Poor little girl! On many occasions she has seen others pet dogs without being bitten, and yet she herself has never been able to do so. "I suppose dogs like others but they just don't like me," she sighs. "I am not wanted."

Here's another example. Imagine that you get a gift for the person you love with all of your heart and upon giving it to them they reply, "Aww! That's so sweet of you. I really appreciate your thoughtfulness. But don't worry, you can keep it."

To all appearances, it seems as if the person you love is just incredibly rude. But are they trying to be rude? Or is it that they are being their normal self? True, their normal is abnormal, but they are not trying to be mean or rude. In their mind they really believe you love them unconditionally and all, as weird as that may be to them, but they don't know how to respond to that. It is not normal to them. They only know how to respond to rejection so that is what they do. They don't consciously think, "I will act like they rejected me even though they just accepted me." They don't even realize they are acting like you reject them. To them, they are just being normal.

"Aww! That's so sweet of you. I really appreciate your thoughtfulness. But *don't worry*, you can keep it." Don't worry?

Can you now discern why they said this? Their mind, coming from the perspective of all of their past experiences, has subconsciously determined that no one really accepts them and wants to give them anything for free. Their belief system has been led to believe a lie; therefore, they say, "Don't worry, you can keep it."

In their mind they have never really been accepted before, and so they never expect it. Rather, they always expect rejection because that is all they've ever received, and therefore, they act like they will be rejected.

If you were to ask them, they would not necessary know why they said this. This is because of all the stuff that goes on in their subconscious. Their rejection file subconsciously updates itself, comes to a subconscious conclusion of the information it receives, and then spits back the information it has gathered. To us, it appears as nasty and rude, but to them, they don't even know why they said what they said. Some people may understand why, because they are half-conscious of what's going on in their mind, but not everybody will know why.

The reason that they said, "Don't worry, you can keep it," is because their brain has already calculated that you want something back from them for your gift, and since they can't pay you for it, they reassure you that you don't have to give them anything for free. In other words, they're saying, "Look, I know you want me to pay you for this gift, but since I cannot pay you for it, I want you to keep it because then you won't lose in the exchange. I don't want to rob you because I love you; therefore, please keep your gift."

They do *not* realize that this is what they are saying, because this

16

is a subconscious up-chuck of information from their rejection file. They do not mean to say this, nor are they conscious of the fact that this is what they are saying. This is their subconscious response to your offer of love. Don't feel offended or hurt by their response, for in reality, they are only loving you in the best way they can by keeping you from losing out in the trade.

It is clear how feelings of rejection can alter the belief system of the emotionally wounded. The rejected individual has been trained to see the world from a different perspective than anyone else. He cannot see eye to eye with others in certain areas because his past experience is different from theirs. Once his belief system has jumped off the rail and is firmly established in the ground, it can be extremely difficult to get back on track. That belief system, once marred, causes a great deal of difficulty, not only for the one rejected but even for those who accept him.

Now do you see how the brain's subconscious reaction to emotional pain can cause problems? Do you see how the process works? First comes feelings of emotional discomfort, then information concerning this incident is subconsciously stored in the mind, the file is subconsciously updated, there is a subconscious conclusion made of the information gathered, and then a subconscious response is given to keep the individual from experiencing emotional pain again.

First comes feelings of emotional discomfort, then information concerning this incident is subconsciously stored...

Not everything happens in the subconscious. It is true that violated individuals make a conscious choice to remember painful incidents, gather the

17

information that can be acquired, and learn how to avoid the pain. But the point to be made is that many things go on in the subconscious that we don't so much as even take thought for. We don't think, "Ouch! This coal is hot. Let me remove my finger." No; this is done subconsciously. We may be half aware of what is going on but not aware enough to see our mistake and keep ourselves from making it once again.

These are just a few examples that show how the rejection process works. The possible resulting outcomes for a rejected individual are just as numerous if not more so than the ways in which he can be emotionally hurt. If only we knew why our friends and loved ones do what they do, oh how much more patient and sympathetic we would be toward them.

The Filter

When dealing with rejection, it is important to note that rejection is *not* what initiates the rejection process. Someone can be completely, unconditionally accepted by another, and yet the rejection process can still begin. Again, rejection does *not* initiate the rejection process. The rejection process is initiated when an individual *feels* rejected.

If only we knew why our friends and loved ones do what they do, oh how much more patient and sympathetic we would be toward them.

In terms of rejection, when we are talking to someone, in all reality, it doesn't matter what we *mean* to say. What matters is what we actually *say*. But then again, it really doesn't matter what we say, it matters what they *hear*. And still further, it doesn't matter what they hear, it matters what they *understand*. And finally, it matters not what they understand, because everything hinges on how it makes them *feel*. If they feel hurt, they are hurt. That is their reality. It doesn't matter how much you accept them in your heart, if they feel emotionally hurt by what you said or did, then their brain senses an intruder. It detects that the emotional being of the individual has been violated and it will set in action that which is necessary to divert and avoid further pain, or at least, to make it hurt less.

> *When dealing with rejection, it is important to note that rejection is not what initiates the rejection process. ... The rejection process is initiated when an individual feels rejected.*

This is why it is so critical that our dealings with each other be fine and sensitive. If the tone in our voice, the look on our face, the roughness with which we move about, or the very atmosphere that surrounds our presence, if any of these speaks to another in an offensive, intruding, or violating way, then we have wounded them, regardless of whether or not they make a conscious note of it.

This is also why it can be so difficult to get someone to feel accepted by you after their belief system has been severely dislodged and grounded out of place. Because they expect rejection, when you do accept them, they still feel rejected. Not because you rejected them, but because their distorted vision interpreted your acceptance of them as nothing more than a sly form of rejection. It is grandly difficult to cause these people to feel loved, not because they are rebellious and obstinate but because all love and understanding is interpreted by their brain as that which causes them emotional pain.

Self-Rejection

It is one thing to be rejected by others, but it is another thing to reject yourself. Self-rejection is when an individual comes to the point of rejecting herself as the result of being rejected by others. It is the most dangerous of all forms of rejection, the strongest one to destroy people, and the most difficult to get out of because it is inflicted by the individual herself.

Self-rejection is one of the ways the brain deals with emotional pain. It hurts to be constantly rejected by others, never knowing when

If they feel hurt, they are hurt. That is their reality.

to expect rejection or having any control in the matter when it comes. But self-rejection fixes these problems. If you reject yourself before someone else rejects you, then you beat them to the punch. They can't hurt you, because you have already hurt yourself. You have complete control in the matter, and they can't just up and abuse you whenever they please.

It should now be obvious why self-rejection is a more stable type of rejection for the one suffering under it and why it would, therefore, be more preferable than to be rejected by someone else. Also, what's nice about self-rejection is that it seems to hurt less too.

Most people who get a splinter stuck deep under their skin would much rather pull it out themselves than let someone else do it. Why? When your finger has a splinter in it, *you* feel the pain. You know just how gentle you need to be to get the splinter out with the least amount of pain possible. Someone else, who doesn't know how much it hurts, would have the tendency to be a little bit more rough than you would, not because they want to hurt you but because they aren't feeling the pain every time they poke and stab you with a needle or tweezers. If someone else removes the splinter from your finger, you can do nothing but helplessly anticipate the next surge of pain. But when you are removing that splinter, there is no stress of anticipation because you know exactly when to expect pain—when you poke yourself! In a case like this, you are your own best sympathizer, so to speak.

Self-rejection is usually initialized either right before or right after rejection hits an individual. If one anticipates that she is about to be rejected in a certain way and at a certain point, self-rejection will cause her to quickly reject herself on that specific point before someone else rejects her on it. Either that, or after a person is rejected upon a certain point, they will then make a decision to reject themselves right then and there on that point so that way they have full control of the issue before it comes back to attack them again.

The saddest part about self-rejection is that it is still rejection; it is still emotional pain. True, it doesn't seem to hurt as much, and yes you do have far more control, but you cannot be happy living this way. Yes, you may be somewhat happy, but your potential level of happiness is drastically lowered. Self-rejection can live as long as life and be as strong as death. Its struggle for preeminence is terrible, and it must be defeated or else there can be little to no true joy in life. Self-rejection, unless dealt with promptly and properly, will only get stronger.

One of the first tell-tale signs that you will often, but not always, notice in someone who is suffering from self-rejection is their denial of the fact that they have suffered a lot of rejection from others. "Oh, I haven't been rejected that much," they'll say. "Sure, I have gone through some junk in life, but I'm okay now. I don't get all worked up about things anymore. If someone rejects me, I don't

Because they expect rejection, when you do accept them, they still feel rejected.

get all emotional over it. I am a 'cold stone' that doesn't experience emotions."

They talk this way because they have learned to turn off their emotional switch. In short, they've learned to reject themselves, for it seems to them that it causes less pain. But this turning off of their emotions is not the way to deal with rejection. Rejection has still done its damage to the heart, and the wound still needs to be healed.

Here is a practical example to show how self-rejection works its way into people's lives and character. Pay close attention and try to see the rejection process in play. Watch for instances of rejection, note the brain's subconscious file updates, the filter, the marring of the belief system, and the rejection habits that are formed to deal with emotional pain. These won't necessarily all be perfectly outlined. You must learn to read people, so study this case, search, and learn.

> *If you reject yourself before someone else rejects you, then you beat them to the punch...*

Sapphire

Sapphire was a very beautiful girl from the day she was born. Her deep blue eyes and rosy red lips gave her father the inspiration for her name: Sapphire Ruby Emerald. Fitting for her name, but rather because she looked like one, all of her friends called her Jewels.

She was a very sweet girl who grew up on the outskirts of a midsized town surrounded by lots of small-scale farmers. She was one of those girls you rarely see in today's world. Her sympathetic love embraced and accepted all, bringing a peace and comfort to many troubled souls. She befriended the friendless and inspired hope in the hopeless. If she ever saw someone who was feeling down, she always attempted to lift them up.

Her parents loved her dearly but were very careful not to spoil her as their only child. She was a very talented girl. From being an excellent pianist, to cooking the most delicious meals, to being able to do small residential plumbing and electrical projects, she seemed able to do it all. But her great talents and abilities did not puff her up with pride.

Of course, Sapphire's life wasn't perfect. Though Sapphire's parents loved her exceedingly, they were not wise in their manner of disciplining her, and therefore, their love for her was blind. Sapphire learned to obey her parents out of fear rather than

The saddest part about self-rejection is that it is still rejection; it is still emotional pain...

love. While a young child, if she in the least showed disobedience or rebellion by word or act, she would hear her mother's words of burning wrath and feel the cruel sting of her father's belt as it wrapped around her tender bottom. She did not hold resentment toward her parents for their harsh treatment. She felt worthy of all the punishment she received as a result of her disobedience and thought that her parents were doing the right thing in keeping her from being a rebel. Besides, didn't it straighten her out and help to make her who she was? But though she thought and felt all this, the look on her daddy's face, expressive of unmerciful anger, witnessed by her while she was being whipped by him, left a deep impression upon her mind.

One major problem that seriously impacted Sapphire's thinking in her later years was that she never had an emotional relationship with her parents. They never taught her as a child to come to them with her emotional joys and sorrows. Their ears were not receptive to her exciting childish experiences, and she did not sense that she had a lap that she could cry into when her heart was broken over her dead puppy. When she sought their love and friendship, she always ran into a cold wall that separated her from her parents. This separation caused a lack of trust between the two parties that made all of their lives harder.

But it must be understood that her parents were not consciously rejecting her. They simply gave to their daughter the only thing they knew. The truth is that both parents suffered from the same rejection they were dishing out to their daughter. They simply did not know how to give her what they themselves had never received as children.

As for Sapphire's natural and acquired talents and capabilities, her efforts never seemed good enough for her parents. Her father always criticized her at the keyboard. "Why Sapph?! Why? You almost played it perfectly and then you blew it right at the end. Why can't you play it like Mozart or something?" She always heard that she could have and should have done better. From critical put downs such as, "Well that was stupid of you. You should know better than to underline with a marker. Now you've ruined the whole book!" to more subtle rejection such as, "The pie you made was great. All except for that one bitter apple seed it was perfect." Once, upon receiving her grade report, her parents jumped on her, "Straight A's in every class but algebra!? Why couldn't you have worked harder and been the first girl in your school to get a perfect report card?! We've taught you to be perfect in everything since you were a baby, but you still don't get it, do you?"

Sapphire's parents knew that she was more advanced than all of the other youth her age, and in some things she was even more advanced than them. They reasoned that this was the result of their pushing her so hard, and they were correct to a great degree. But their never-satisfied attitude and rapid, unwarranted pushing and shoving drove Sapphire so fast that her emotions were not able to keep up with her at times. Several nights every month she would bury her face in her pillow and drench it with her tears, wondering why she could never do anything right. "Why am I such a failure?" she would sob. "I always do my best, but everything always messes up."

Aside from her parents, Sapphire received disappointed looks and remarks from all of her family, friends, and teachers, along with all of their subtle criticisms. Her family was disappointed with what she wanted to accomplish in life, her teachers in her completed homework assignments, and her friends in her love for innocent recreation and her refusal to engage with them in their poor choice of activities.

As Sapphire moved into her later teens, things grew worse. She was always being misunderstood by her friends, many of whom began misjudging her motives. For example, she once purchased a gift of ice cream and a card for her dearest friend Carrie who always seemed stressed and depressed and was quick to lose her temper. In the card, which had a cute little doggie on the front, she jokingly wrote, "Because I know you often get hot-headed… I thought this gift might cool you off!" She joyfully wrote her message while thinking of how it would put a smile on the face of her often despairing and troubled friend. Sapphire had always loved Carrie. She was always trying to help her, and she had never done a single thing to injure her. Therefore, she had no inclination that Carrie would mistake her gift of thoughtful love for anything but that. This was Sapphire's way of telling Carrie, in a joking sort of way, "I accept and love you for who you are, even though you get upset and go off on me at times."

Sapphire asked another friend to deliver the gift, so it wasn't until way later that she found out that her gift had been misinterpreted. She found out about the problem when she gave Carrie a call to see how she was doing. Carrie answered, and after Sapphire said hello, Carrie hung up. Wondering what happened, Sapphire called back. This time Carrie's mother answered the phone. "Hello!"

Sapphire responded, "This is Sapphire, Carrie's friend. Is Carrie there?"

Carrie's mom answered, "Well, I am Carrie's mother, and she doesn't want to talk to you."

Wow! What a surprise! Sapphire quickly called one of Carrie's friends to see if she knew what was wrong. When Carrie's friend mentioned the gift and card, everything came together, and it all made sense. Instead of receiving the message that Sapphire was meaning to give, Carrie got the message: "Man, you've got a problem. You really need to lose that bad temper. Here is some ice cream to cool down that hot head of yours." And so, in trying to help, Sapphire was accused and wrongly judged as trying to hurt her friend.

But you can't blame it all on Carrie. Carrie had suffered much rejection in her life, and as a result, she began to look at everything through the crippling glasses of rejection. All things meant for her good were taken negatively because she had experienced so much negativity that she never expected anything else.

At a different time, Sapphire tried to surprise another one of her friends by washing her friend's car while she was out. But unfortunately, her friend returned before she could finish and started fussing at her. "Hey! Stop that! My parents are going to think I'm lazy. Stop trying to make yourself look like the perfect daughter."

Whenever Sapphire saw her friends taking a course that would only bring them unhappiness, she tried to reason with them and give them wise advice to keep them away from trouble and punishment. She didn't want to see them get hurt. But they just got upset with her, "Why do you always have to disagree and cause controversy? We know you think you know everything and are all perfect and all, but you're not. Stop messing up our plans. If you aren't going to help, then don't say anything."

The friction between her and her friends got to such a point that it seemed that if Sapphire said or did anything trouble broke out. Once upon entering the cafeteria where her friends were, they all, sitting at their favorite lunch table, discontinued their happy chatter, put on serious faces, and whispered among themselves, "Shhhhh! Stop talking. Miss Perfect is here." The message that Sapphire received from this incident was, "Even by your presence you ruin everyone's fun."

It must be understood that Sapphire's friends never meant to hurt her as they did. They still loved her very much even though they didn't get along anymore like they used to. And often their comments toward her, though inexcusable, were a result of their own feelings of rejection.

Something else that seriously gnawed at Sapphire's enduring stamina also had its origin with her friends. They had been trying for years to get Sapphire to "loosen up" and not be so "extreme" in her fidelity to principle and proper conduct. After being together with her friends for so many years, she slowly began to become like them in character.

The sad truth of the matter is that after Sapphire softened a little bit in her behavior toward them, they received from Sapphire the treatment they had been giving to her, and they didn't like it. "Jewels!" they cried, "What happened to you? You're just not the nice girl you used to be."

Sapphire, of course, was startlingly shocked. *What is going on?* she wondered. *My friends have been on my case for years about getting me to become more like them, and now that I imperceptibly have, they want me to be the 'nice girl' again.* In a sorrowful fit of rage, she asked herself, "Can't they just make up their mind?"

All of these little things—her parents disappointment, dissatisfaction, and criticism; her friends misjudgment of her motives, gifts, and entreaties of love and their remarks of disapproval for her tight or loose conduct; and the fact that everything she did seemed to cause a problem—wore down her spirit and placed a crushing burden upon her very being.

The sprouting of the straw that proverbially broke Sapphire's back had its beginnings when her and her friend Ron went to the river early one Sunday morning with three youthful acquaintances who seemed very friendly. Sapphire had had a difficult time bringing herself to go to the river with her friends. She suffered so much from rejection that she started becoming quite comfortable with it. It was actually becoming easier for her to just accept that she was rejected and live accordingly. She felt that it was easier for her to simply decline the invitation than to risk being hurt by her friends while she was there. Another thing that caused her hesitation was that she was very afraid that somehow she would mess everybody's day up if she went. Nevertheless, she went.

It just so happened that while Sapphire was sitting by the river's edge she saw a honeybee hovering over some saturated sand in an effort to sip some water. Sapphire had absolutely adored honeybees from childhood, and she was sad when she saw them suffering. It caused tears to well up in her eyes when she had to put one out of its misery. She thought they were cute and adorable with their little fuzzy bodies, and she loved how they buzzed as they went about in search of nectar.

Ron was sitting next to her, and upon seeing the bee, he quickly picked up a rock and smashed it. Sapphire went berserk. "What in the world did you do that for!?" she cried at Ron as she gently shoved him with her hand.

Unfortunately for both of them, Ron was off balance at the moment of her shove, and he fell over. In the process, his cell phone, which had been resting on his knee, fell into the water. "My phone! My phone!" he cried as he snatched his phone out of the river's edge.

Sapphire now felt absolutely miserable. "I knew that if I came I would ruin someone's day," she sobbed. "And all over a honeybee." She now wished she had never been born; then she couldn't be such a curse to humanity. She now wished that there was a dark hole in the ground that would just swallow her up. She felt totally wretched the rest of the day. In spite of her negative feelings, the five of them spent the whole day swimming and were totally exhausted by the time they headed home as the sun was going down.

On the way back, Sapphire and Ron's three new friends decided to stop at a store to check out some flashlights they had seen previously. "We'll be really quick. We promise!" the oldest one said as he released a genuinely sincere smile that somehow faintly resembled a mischievous sort of grin.

This gave Sapphire the willies. "Okay!" Sapphire replied, getting over her chills. "But hurry up! I can't be hanging around in a car with Ron at nine o'clock at night." And so Sapphire and Ron waited in the back seat of the car. Rather rapidly, both of them, being thoroughly exhausted from their fourteen-hour day, fell into a deep sleep.

They didn't wake up until the next morning when Sapphire's father knocked on the car window. Upon hearing her father's sharp knocking, Sapphire quickly jumped. Quite startled, she wondered where she was. A quick glance around the more than half empty car, at Ron's frightened facial expression, and then at her father's solemn and frowning face told her that she was busted.

"Ron!" her father said after she opened the car door, "I believe you should be getting home now. I'll be talking to you later, but right now I need to have a little discussion with my daughter." The tone in her father's voice told her and Ron that explanations would be of no avail now.

On the way home, Sapphire received one of the sharpest tongue-lashings she had ever heard. She knew that attempting to explain what had happened would be useless while her father was so upset, and so she remained silent until after they had reached home and he had finally calmed down. She then explained to both of her parents in detail exactly what had happened.

"So what became of your new friends then?" her mother asked.

"I don't know," Sapphire exclaimed. "I want to know just as much as you do." Sapphire's parents didn't believe her story though they were dying to and tried to as hard as they could. The lack of an emotional relationship with their daughter, which caused alienation between them, inspired this mistrust, and Sapphire felt it in the depths of her being.

In their great efforts to force themselves to believe their daughter, they did not punish her or state their unbelief in her, even though she could feel it in the very atmosphere around them.

Adding to the burdens she already carried in her mind, the thought that her parents believed that she had lied to them and purposefully slept overnight with Ron in his car really hurt. She found herself walking in the park two days later pondering the agonies of her heart. "Why can't I ever do anything right?" she whispered to herself. "I always mess everything up. My friends misunderstand me, and my parents don't trust me. I do nothing but ruin their lives. Now those people who are dearest to me are known as the parents or friends of a prostitute thanks to the newspapers front page headline, *'Sleeping Beauty; Sapphire lost and found.'* Every time I speak or act somebody gets hurt or something goes wrong. I can't even walk into a room without making people feel uncomfortable! I'm nothing but a curse to humanity. If I can't be a blessing to the world, then why bother living? Oh how I hate myself."

What Sapphire desperately needed at this moment in her life was to feel special, loved, wanted, needed, appreciated, missed, thought about, cared for, yearned for, sought after, and cried over. She needed to know that she couldn't be lived without and that she meant everything to someone. Sadly, everywhere she turned for help looked hopeless. Nobody seemed to want her. If she would have had a close emotional relationship with her friends or family, she would have gone directly to those who would sympathize with her in her grief and speak words of love and affirmation to her troubled soul. She did not have this connection with her parents because they didn't know how to give it, having never received it themselves as children.

And she didn't have this type of relationship with any of her friends. Whenever she sought their sympathy and tried to unravel the burdens of her heart to them, they would quickly cut her off by saying stuff such as, "Oh, you shouldn't be worrying about such small things. It is ridicules to let such little things bother you so much." Thus, her feelings were denied, her pain belittled, her person rejected, and her hope for sympathetic love quenched. These words were the last thing she needed to hear in her time of distress.

What she needed was to hear words of acceptance and tender sympathy such as, "Oh, I'm so sorry dear. I understand your troubles; I've gone through the same type of thing. But don't be disheartened. I love you, and you mean the world to me. It hurts me to see you in such pain. Cheer up! Everything will be okay." But these words of assurance, affirmation, cheer, and tender love, which would have proven to be a lifeline, were never spoken to her dying heart.

31

It was near the end of Sapphire's morning walk that she made her decision in a fit of faint anger and desperate despair. "If my friends don't want me around, I'll stay away from and avoid them. If they won't have me the way I was, and they won't have me the way *they wanted me,* then *they will not have me at all!* If every time I speak, something bad happens, I'll only open my mouth to eat. People can talk to themselves if they want to talk to someone. If every time I try to be nice to others, I'm misunderstood and abused, I'll stop trying to be nice. They can be nice to themselves. I am simply not wanted. That's right, Sapphire, you are simply not wanted; you are worthless." Sapphire began to really like the idea of not being wanted. It just felt so... good.

After applying her plan for a few days, for the purpose of avoiding more rejection, she hurt from not trying to help her friends when they needed it and for flat out ignoring them and walking away when they tried to talk to her. The separation she thought would aid her pain only added to it. "Oh, it doesn't matter what I do!" she cried. "I am always WRONG!"

The ripened straw that was so soon to crush her spirit to the utmost fell on her during her last, but now, regular despairing walk through the park. Added to all of her other woes was the pressing burden of guilt for certain things she had done in her life. This burden was among the heaviest she had to bear. It clawed at her heart like a rabid lion and from it she could find no rest. As she slowly crept along through the park, she came across a small boy who was crying as he sat by a tree trying to pull a large splinter out of his hand. Sapphire's heart sparked with hope as it went out in sympathy to this poor child. *Finally*, she thought to herself, *somebody who needs me and will want my help.*

She knelt down and spoke soothing words to the boy while inspecting his wound. Then she quickly took off her backpack and found her tweezers. But the boy, having now wiped the tears from his face, recognized Sapphire and cried out, "Hey! I know you. You're that prostitute girl daddy showed me in the newspaper. Get away from me. I don't want your help." The boy started screaming in a demonic frenzy, "Get away! Get away, you prostitute!"

While the boy continued to scream, Sapphire stood up and slowly backed away, scarcely aware that he was still screaming. It was as if she was now in an alternate reality. She was stunned, shocked, and finally broken. Her life had reached its limit. The fountain of her tears burst, and she ran away, from the boy, her parents, her friends, but mostly, from herself.

After running for a while, blinded by her tears, she eventually stumbled and fell to the ground, clung to it, and in her mind, started screaming to herself, *I can't take it anymore! If this is life then I choose death!*

Gasping for breath, which was controlled by her choking sobs, she tremblingly got up onto her hands and knees with her face still down, inspired and determined by a power outside of herself to quickly find a means to end her life. But...

Chapter 3

Tracing the Process

Examples

It is vitally important that you see the reality of the rejection process and how it works, what it does to people, and also the variableness of the possible outcomes for different individuals who suffer under its tyranny. It seems that the best way to accomplish this is to provide real-life examples you can relate with. It is hard to touch all cases, but hopefully everyone will be able to relate to some degree or another.

The following illustrations are not fictional examples; they are real-life practical experiences presented for you to analyze so that discerning the rejection process and its results will become second nature. After completing this book, your job is to observe those around you and trace the process of rejection in their lives so that you can help them break the cycle.

Mark

Growing up, Mark didn't have many friends. He was kind of a different character who sort of seemed like the oddball in the group. The few friends he did have he treasured to the utmost. But sadly for Mark, his friends did not seem to value him to the same degree.

Mark's friends never seemed to call, e-mail, write, or try to spend time with him. The only e-mails that Mark ever received from his friends seemed to be the ones they wrote when they felt guilty for not writing in so long or to simply shut him up for being so persistent in trying to get a response from them. The only way he was able to do anything with his friends was if *he* called them up and said something like, "Hey, lets do such and such, at such and such a time." But even these precious appointed moments for Mark were often cast off as if somebody or something else was always more important than him. Mark soon began to feel like an old, used toy that was boring and had been put on the top shelf. He began to feel as if his friends were his friends but he was not theirs.

One time, he made an appointment to go hiking with a friend on the Blue Ridge Parkway. They planned to go the following morning and were going to meet at a certain lookout. But when Mark arrived the next morning at the lookout, he noticed that his always-early friend was not yet there. He waited for half an hour, figuring his friend had once again deserted him at the last moment, and Mark ended up hiking by himself.

Upon returning home, Mark called his friend and asked why he hadn't shown up. "Oh! I'm sorry," his friend answered. "Somebody called me right after I got off the phone with you yesterday. He wanted me to go to the mall with him and some of his other friends. I figured you wouldn't mind, so I decided to go with him."

Mark wasn't upset, just a little confused. "So why didn't you call and tell me?" Mark asked. "I would have understood."

"Oh, sorry," his friend replied, "I forgot!"

Repeated and continued instances such as this, and similar to it, caused Mark to feel unwanted, but he did not give up. He continued to make plans with his friends, and they continued to let him down. He continued to e-mail his friends who never wrote back, and he continued to leave messages on his friends' voicemail. He, like many others, felt rejection from those he loved most.

Today, Mark has friends who e-mail him because they want to and who want to do stuff with him, but he constantly pushes them away by implying or saying things such as, "I want you to understand that you don't have to write to me," "Please don't feel obligated to email me," "I don't want you to see it as a necessity to do things with me," or "If you want to stop writing to me and doing stuff together with me, you can. You don't have to feel bad about it. I will understand."

In response to Mark's statements, his friends feel rejected by him. "Why does he always act like we don't want him in our lives?" they wonder. Their only explanation for Mark's behavior is 1) "He is just weird" or 2) "Perhaps Mark acts like this because we are not wanted in his life, and so he pushes us away."

But is it really because Mark is weird and doesn't want them that he behaves that way? Or is it because, in his eyes, he has been so neglected and rejected that he insists that something must be wrong when his friends accept him? Because of this, he tries to fix the nonexistent problem by giving them a message of assurance, "It's okay if you'd rather me be out of your life; I'll understand. But please don't pretend to accept me when you would much rather have nothing to do with me. I don't want to be something extra that sucks your time and attention that you have to deal with and stress over. If I am going to be that to you, then I simply would rather not be. It's okay if you want me out of your life; I'll still love you anyway."

The same reason Mark gives this message to his friends is the same reason he avoids spending time with them. "Why don't you come over here and spend time with us?" they ask him. "Why are you always off in some secluded room or hiding in some secret corner?"

"Because I don't want to bother you," Mark replies.

"Why do you always feel like you are a bother to us? It is really not nice to look at your friends as being bothered by you when we want you involved with us. You act like we don't care about you. Why do you do that?" they ask.

This is when Mark remains silent. He fears to tell them he really doesn't believe they want him as their friend. This would be like slapping them in the face. But at the same time, he really truly and honestly just doesn't comprehend that they want him as their friend. He doesn't believe that his friends are lying to him—he knows they would never do that. But the past rejection in his life, being built upon and confirmed for nearly eighteen years, is of much greater magnitude in his mind than his friend's acceptance, and he just doesn't *really* believe that he is accepted by them. How could that be possible? His silence in response to his friend's question proves the greatest means of separating him from them. But what can he do? He either slaps them in the face by answering their question, or he slaps them in the face by his silence.

He never experienced acceptance as he needed to, so when it presents itself, he chooses rejection, not so much because it is enjoyable, but because that is all he has ever known—cold water.

The fact that Mark really doesn't feel accepted by his friends is also the reason that he doesn't call them on the phone. One of his friends asked him, "Why don't you ever call and talk to me?"

"Because I figure that you are probably busy or have something more important to do then talk to me," Mark answered.

"Well, I think that the reason is because you really just don't want to talk to me," his friend replied. "You show me this same attitude all the time. If you really wanted to talk with me, then I think you would find a way to do so."

Mark's friend has good reason to believe what she does. From her perspective, this is what she really sees. But she doesn't understand Mark's past. She doesn't know about Mark's longing to speak with her, and because she doesn't know of it, she doesn't believe it. If she can't see him express a desire to speak with her by actually calling, then as far as she is concerned, it doesn't exist. But again, what can Mark do to clear up the misunderstanding? He has spoken honestly to her, and she won't believe him, and he finds it nearly impossible to call her because he is a slave of rejection.

To help us better understand where Mark is coming from, let us look at it this way. A child, born and raised in cold water, who has never felt or experienced the sensation of warmth doesn't comprehend the concept of warm water. He will avoid it and cling to his cold water because he knows what to expect. Though it may sound like something he wants, the thought of warm water is uncertain and frightening. Warm water to him is change, and we as humans are uneasy about change. And so the child will remain in his uncomfortable cold water because he knows what to expect.

So it is in Mark's case. He never experienced acceptance as he needed to, so when it presents itself, he chooses rejection, not so much because it is enjoyable, but because that is all he has ever known— cold water.

How could you expect someone who was blind from birth to comprehend the color blue? How could you expect Mark to understand that he is accepted when, in his mind, it isn't possible? Hadn't he looked for acceptance like diamonds in a mine and never found it? How is it then that somebody is just freely giving it to him now?

For Mark to believe that someone really accepts him unconditionally would be like us really believing the flashing pop-up on our computer screen that says "YOU'VE JUST WON $1,000,000!!! CLICK HERE TO RECEIVE YOUR CA$H!!!" I am sure all of us have said, in utter sarcasm, "Yeah right. Oh yay. Now I'm rich." This offer has appeared so many times. We win a million dollars every six months, and it's *always* a lie. Why should we believe the pop-up ad this time? Now do you see where Mark is coming from? Do you blame him for being pessimistic?

Mark had been rejected again and again. It has become normal to him to be rejected. He has come to expect rejection, and therefore, he acts like he is or will be rejected. This acting as if he expects rejection ends up causing him to be rejected even more, but he's not weird or stupid. He's normal, considering the circumstances of his life experiences. And shall we not be sympathetic toward him?

Rachel

Rachel, as a twelve-year-old girl, was with her mother in Walmart one day doing some much-needed grocery shopping. In the dry cereal aisle, her mother happened to glance at Rachel whose long straight blond hair was fluttering about her head. Irritated that Rachel hadn't taken extra special care to make sure she appeared neat and tidy in public, her mother belted out, "Rachel Elisabeth Smith! What is your problem, child? Your hair is a mess. People are going to laugh at you with your hair like that, and you're going to embarrass me!"

Rachel, startled at the rapid change in her mother's attitude, immediately attempted to fix her hair, cautiously looking about to make sure no one else had seen her.

Rachel's mother not only subtly, though unintentionally, injured her daughter with her own rejection but she also placed a fear in Rachel's mind that other people, upon seeing her imperfect hair, will make fun of and reject her. Similar instances such as this one shaped

Rachel's life. Remarks such as, "Rachel! You're going to embarrass me with that spot on your blouse," and "Who knows what people are going to think of you if you go walking around town with that spinach between your teeth," have not made Rachel's life a happier one.

Now, Rachel wakes up at 4:30 a.m. five days a week to make it to work on time at 8:30 in the morning. The sad thing is that her work is only one block down the street. You can probably guess what Rachel spends her time doing. After a thirty-minute breakfast, she spends approximately the next three hours (which should be spent sleeping) in the bathroom brushing her hair, cleaning her teeth, washing her face, making sure she doesn't have any zits, checking for stains on her clothes, making sure she doesn't look fat in her chosen outfit, determining if her clothes match, etc.

She does all of this because she is afraid that if she doesn't look perfect she will be rejected by her boss, friends, family, and even her husband. But it is not necessary for anyone to spend three hours every day sprucing themselves up in order to be accepted.

> *If the nasty tyrant can hit someone very hard and very fast, it will gleefully watch as its prey, struggling, breathes its last.*

Rachel's mother wasn't trying to be critical and faultfinding with her daughter, and she certainly never meant for it to so negatively affect her daughter's life. All she wanted was for Rachel to escape the rejection she had faced as a youth. But her way of accomplishing this was unwise. If only she had calmly said things more along the lines of, "Dear, your hair is out of place. Do you think you can fix it?" And if she had left out the part about what others might think, the far-reaching results may not have been so bad.

Rachel's mother didn't mean for her daughter to feel rejected by her, but what Rachel's mother meant was not what was important at the moment of criticism. What mattered was how Rachel felt. Have you ever heard of the saying, "What you gave doesn't matter, it's what they got that counts"? Or the one that goes, "What you said doesn't matter, but what they understood does"? Do you perceive the truth of these sayings? Rachel felt rejection, and this seed of rejection produced its evil fruit.

Now, it wasn't Rachel's mother alone who helped form her daughters extreme habit. Comments in her childhood such as, "Hey zit face!" and statements in her teen years like, "You look like you've gained a few pounds," coupled with the question of, "Are you pregnant?" all aided in developing Rachel's unhealthy regard for her appearance.

Rachel is well aware of the reason for her habit of spending hours every morning primping. In fact, she knows exactly why she does it. "I want other people to accept me," she says. This is a fitting example of conscious behavior development.

Do you find yourself stuck in a similar race for acceptance from people? Do you see it as next to impossible to change your bad habits?

Emily

Emily received rebukes, put downs, and sharp criticisms for *seemingly* anything and everything in her life. These things included how she looked, how she did things, and what opinions she held.

One day Emily went to the airport to pick up a friend who she hadn't seen in a long time. Upon seeing each other, they embraced. After their embrace, her friend said to her, "Wow! You look a lot different than you used to."

Emily was hurt. But why? Her friend didn't mean it in a negative

41

way. Unfortunately, throughout her whole life, everything has always *seemed* to come to her in a negative form. She interprets her friend's word "different" as "worse," even though her friend never said anything about better or worse. All her friend said was "different." But for Emily, who views the world through her rejection glasses, the word "d-i-f-f-e-r-e-n-t" reads with sharp clarity "w-o-r-s-e."

This is why we, in our conversing with others, need to consider with whom we are dealing and be very careful in our selection of words. If Emily's friend had told her, "Wow! You look a lot *better* than you used to," Emily would have probably figured that her friend was just saying that to be nice. She might have even turned around and said something like, "Look, you don't have to say that to make me feel good. Just tell me the truth. I'm not going to be hurt."

Emily was hurt when her friend said that she looked different, but if her friend had said that she looked better, Emily would have told her to be honest, say that she looked worse, and that she wouldn't be hurt with this "truth" as she saw it. But the fact of the matter is that she would be hurt. Emily was hurt by the word "different," and so the word "worse" would just as much, if not more so, cause her pain. Why, then, would Emily insist that she wouldn't be hurt? The reason is because Emily has learned to turn off her emotions as rejection hits her, so it honestly doesn't *seem* to hurt her so much. Here is an illustration to make this easier to understand.

If someone is often stung by honeybees, let's say a beekeeper or someone who works around beehives, one of two things will happen: 1) he will either become more and more allergic to the stings with increased allergic reactions, or 2) he will become more and more "immune" to the stings to where he has no allergic reactions to them and the sharp burn lasts for only a few seconds, if that.

Emily, stung countless times by rejection, has become "immune" to it. But this does not mean that she is not injured. The stinger and poison are still injected into her and still have their damaging effects, just like a physical honeybee stinger and poison do. But to Emily, this sting is not as painful as it used to be. She will avoid it if at all possible, but if she is stung she takes it quietly, silently, to where perhaps no one but herself knows about it.

On the other hand, looking back at a previous example, although Sapphire seemed to build up some sort of tolerance to it, she seemed to become more allergic to the sting of rejection until all it took was a small prick from a little boy to nearly result in her death. In some cases, neither

> *The victim of hopelessness and despair will frantically grasp for some sort of control in his life, and therefore, he lays his hands on rejection, that which to him has been the ruling power in his life.*

allergic reaction build up or immunization have as much opportunity to take place. Even if somebody has never been stung by a honeybee before in their life, too many stings at once can result in the death of the victim. So it is with rejection. If the nasty tyrant can hit someone very hard and very fast, it will gleefully watch as its prey, struggling, breathes its last.

This, in a sense, also hit Sapphire. The pain of past rejection became present rejection pain, and these, in connection with that last sting, nearly killed her. For her it was too much. It must be remembered that feelings of rejection do not die easily. They live on, though seemingly dormant at times, and come back to haunt and harass its victim.

Jacob

Jacob can testify to how the turning off of emotions, as in the case of Emily, is true. Here is his story.

Jacob had known a certain girl for quite a while. They were friends though they didn't spend that much time together. Jacob loved and cared for her very much and did everything he possibly could to make her life a happier one.

One day she received a message from him telling her of his great concern for her due to different reasons and circumstances he had gathered. She was sharp and noticed in his message that he cared for her as more than just a friend, although it was never his purpose to reveal this to her so soon. As a result, she wrote to him to make things clear.

In her letter she said that she was seeing a "gentleman" and that they both liked each other, though they weren't doing anything about it yet. The "yet" in her letter implied that they would do something about it in the future. Jacob read her letter and was like, "Okay, cool!" He wasn't upset. He didn't *feel* very hurt. After all, all he wanted was for her to be happy, and if she was happier without him, then he was all the happier for her.

The second day after reading her letter, Jacob got off work, drove to a nice shady place, parked the car, started thinking, and began to cry. He again felt his foe—rejection—even though it was never meant to be such. His beloved friend never meant to hurt him. Jacob had loved her unselfishly. He did not request, require, or expect anything in return for his love to her. He loved her for one reason, simply because *she was*.

But Jacob's heart, like everyone else's, longed to be loved, and when the target of his love didn't love him back, his heart sank. He was crushed; he was broken. His greatest joys had faded; his purest hopes had died. He had never cried out for a return of love, but its open refusal pierced his heart like a barbed poisoned arrow, truly aimed. Oh how his heart ached for a return of love from the object of his! His love for her had not changed; it's just that the picture of her, which had so often cheered his heart, now caused it to cry in mournful tones of deepest sorrow.

Jacob did not feel hurt for about two days after being rejected. This was because he had been hurt by rejection so much in his life that he had learned to turn off his emotions and say to himself, "Oh well. That's life." He had learned to reject himself and take away the opportunity of others to reject him. But his emotions eventually caught up with him as he sat in the car.

When acceptance has once again *seemed* to refuse to lay hold of someone after repeated instances of rejection, rejection itself may *seem* to be the only thing left to grab onto. The victim of hopelessness and despair will frantically grasp for some sort of control in his life, and therefore, he lays his hands on rejection, that which to him has been the ruling power in his life. He treasures his new best friend rejection, who, in his mind, has never disappointed him and has never let him down. He clings to it for dear life while attempting to bury forever the hope and desire for acceptance.

This was the case with Jacob. Forever did he want to lock out all opposite gender relationships from his life, never to seek them again. The temptation to do so was incredibly strong. The pain of rejection was just too much for him. Since in his eyes he had never been accepted in his life, he would be utterly delighted to choose rejection. At least then he would have some say, some control in his life. Nobody could then reject him anymore, because he then would have taken that ability from them in that he rejected himself.

At a certain point of rejection in life, one's thoughts may well be something along these lines, "I'm sick of acceptance; I've had enough! Since acceptance won't take hold of me, then I want nothing to do with it, and when it comes my way, I will utterly reject it. And I will do this for the rest of my life… Period!"

But to the ones who speak these unspoken words to themselves, I say, You are not really angry at acceptance. You are angry at rejection because it has withheld acceptance from you. Don't blame and punish acceptance for what rejection has done by refusing it and hardening your heart against it once it comes your way. Acceptance is the innocent party that tried to help and bring comfort, hope and cheer, while rejection has always sought to malign, torture, and destroy. If you must be infuriated, direct your wrath at rejection.

Joe

Joe grew up in a family where criticism was a daily part of life. Joe was a responsible boy who never procrastinated and always tried to do his best. But no matter how soon he finished his chores or how precisely they had been completed, he could never seem to please his mother. "Can't you wash those dishes any faster? You're so slow," she would say. "Just get out of the way, I'll do them." Or he would hear something like, "If you can't get the dishes any cleaner than this, you might as well just stop washing them because you're wasting your time."

His father also criticized his yard work responsibilities. "You know, son," he would say, looking over the top of his newspaper and reading glasses, "if you had only … then … would have looked better," or "If you just … then you could have finished sooner."

Besides his critical parents, Joe's boss at work really turned on the heat. His boss would often stand behind him looking over his shoulder at how he was accomplishing his tasks. Let's take a look at a likely

46

day for Joe at work.

One day Joe's boss said, "Can I ask what you're doing?"

"Painting the bedroom doorjambs like you told me to," Joe replied.

"But the thing is," his boss explained, "we don't have all week to paint a few jambs. Just go and finish washing the grout off the tile. I'll finish painting."

After a few minutes of washing tile, Joe's boss came in behind him and after a few seconds of silence asked, "Why are you washing the tile like that?"

"Because this is how you showed me to do it yesterday," Joe answered.

"But today we are working on an unfinished house," his boss replied. "Don't worry about making it look so clean. Don't you ever use your head?"

Later that day Joe was replacing some cedar siding on the house. Joe's boss came around the corner and said, "Why in the world are you using that dinky hammer for nailing up those boards?"

"Because this is the only hammer I could find in the truck, and I figured it would work since you used it for this siding the other day," Joe answered.

"Yeah, but if you can't hit those nails harder than that, you either need to find another hammer or come and get mine. But whatever!" his boss said in a huff. "Come and help me clean up inside so we can finish for the day."

After gathering the tools together and throwing out all the garbage, Joe started to carefully sweep the new hardwood floor in such a way as to not stir up all the drywall dust and to avoid getting it on the new furniture. "Why are you sweeping so slowly?" Joe's boss asked.

"I don't want this white dust to get all over their dark furniture," Joe replied.

His boss sighed, "Sweep faster, and don't worry about the dust."

Joe began to sweep faster, still trying to be careful with the dust. But despite Joe's efforts, dust started to get into the air and onto everything. "What is your problem, Joe?" his boss bolted. "You're getting dust on everything!"

"But you told me not to worry about the dust, just to sweep faster," Joe answered.

"Forget what I said," his boss barked. "Can't you see this mess? Didn't you think to be careful?"

Joe, quite perplexed, stood there with a blank expression on his face and tried to apologize for the mess.

Such was Joe's life at work. He wasn't an experienced finisher, but his boss always seemed to expect him to work as if he had done finish work for thirty years or so. Joe, always seeking to do his best, began trying to anticipate what his boss wanted in his work and reason like his boss would as to the best way to accomplish his appointed tasks. But he soon began to get tired of attempting to anticipate his boss's expectations and reasoning like him when he found that his boss could always find something wrong with either the way he worked or the work itself.

She felt emotionally hurt, and therefore, she was emotionally hurt.

Joe's parents and his boss never meant to negatively affect his life. In fact, all of them thought they were doing Joe a favor by criticizing him, reasoning that it is only by setting high goals and having high expectations and standards that someone excels in life. But this reasoning, in Joe's case, only robbed him of much peace in life.

Today, Joe can't work normally at his job or at other places when somebody is either watching him or he at least thinks they are watching him, especially if that somebody is his boss. If he does think somebody is watching him, he does one of three things: 1) he goes nuts, 2) he tries to work faster and more effectively, or 3) in an attempt to justify himself, he mumbles excuses out loud as to why he can't work right or why his work isn't coming out perfect. Joe also avoids taking his paid fifteen-minute breaks for fear his boss will see him not working and get on his case, even though it is perfectly okay to take his paid breaks. Joe doesn't even feel comfortable in his own home in the presence of his own wife when she helps him with the dishes for fear that she might criticize him in her mind.

Rose

Rose was born flat-footed, along with some other minor foot problems that made it difficult for her to learn to walk. Fortunately, through therapy and proper foot exercises and footwear, she eventually learned to walk perfectly normal with only a slight pain in her feet that she felt every now and then. Her condition continued to improve into her late teens and early twenty's. During these years of her life, Rose's longing to feel accepted by her friends required her, as far as she was concerned, to wear more fashionable footwear. This feeling sprang up based on a statement from one of her best friends. "Rose!" Rebecca exclaimed. "Where did you get those shoes? They look like my grandmother's old farm clogs."

Rebecca, of course, didn't consider how Rose would interpret her statement until the moment after she finished speaking it. Rebecca was just asking an honest question with no harm intended. In fact, she actually liked Rose's "clogs" and wanted to get some for herself. That is what prompted her question. Fearing, however, that Rose might feel hurt by what she had said, Rebecca quickly changed the subject, hoping that Rose would not misunderstand her and take it to heart. But Rebecca's hope was already dead.

Rebecca's question played again and again in Rose's mind like a broken record. "They look like my grandmother's old farm clogs. Rose! Where did you get those shoes? Old farm clogs."

As a result, Rose started wearing shoes that were too narrow for her unusually wide feet, and she even began wearing shoes with one inch higher heels than normal, something her physician had forbidden her to do. You can probably guess that the condition of Rose's feet began to worsen.

Paul, Rose's husband, loved her immensely and was afraid of what Rose's future would be if she continued her unwise course. "Dearest," he said, "please stop wearing those shoes. You don't know how much it breaks my heart to come home and see you all teary-eyed in pain." Rose actually thought that Paul liked seeing her in her fancier shoes. She well knew that he didn't want her to wear them for her health's sake, but she thought that he thought (not very accurate is it) she looked better in these shoes.

Obviously they look way better than grandmother's old farm clogs, she thought. And so, in her mind, for her family's, friend's, and husband's sake, Rose wore shoes that ended up worsening her condition.

From her childhood, Rose had never felt completely accepted by her friends because of her wide, flat feet, even though they were the ones who had stood up for her when others taunted her, crying, "Duck feet! Duck feet! Quack! Quack!" while throwing their sandwich crusts at her. So now, in order to gain the acceptance she thought she never fully had, she caused her friends, family, and even her spouse to fear for her health.

Now, is Rose out of her mind for wearing improper footwear? Can you understand why she does it? Will you jump on her case and tell her how stupid she is? Will doing so fix the problem or make it worse?

Will it make her feel like you accept or reject her?

Rebecca was one of Rose's few friends who actually accepted her for who she was and didn't even so much as request her to change. Rebecca accepted Rose. But regardless of her acceptance, this one misunderstanding made Rose feel rejected. She felt emotionally hurt, and therefore, she was emotionally hurt. And how did this pain affect her actions, for better or for worse?

Mary

Andrew could never understand why on earth his wife, Mary, started balling her eyes out every time he spoke seriously with her. It was a mystery he could not fathom. It's not like he raised his voice or spoke harshly to her with anger upon his lips. All Andrew did was be serious. He often spoke this way when he was calm and settled down from his hectic day. However, he started trying to be much more tender and soft in his manner because of his wife's reaction to him.

One day after he had gone outside to get the mail, he came running in the house crying exuberantly, "Mary Lisa Sands!!! Look at this!!!" He quickly reached out to hand her a check as she collapsed to the floor and started sobbing. "What in the world is the matter, dear?" he said, stooping to lift his wife off the floor. "What happened?"

"I don't know," she choked. "Just please don't call me that."

"Don't call you what?" Andrew wanted to know.

She began to sob harder, "My name!" she cried. "Don't say my name!"

"But dear," Andrew wondered, "I call you by your name all the time. Why did you get upset just now?"

"My full name!" she said, getting control of herself again. "Never say my full name!"

This experience proved to be a key in Andrew's hand to unlock the reason for his wife's emotional breakdowns. Upon discussing this instance with his wife later that evening, he discovered that when Mary was much younger her parents only called her by her full name when hell was about to break loose on her for something she had either said or done wrong. Now, because her full name was associated with such an agony of trauma, every time she hears her full name she bursts into tears. Whenever Andrew got serious about something, he always called his wife by her full name.

In Mary's experience, her full name became associated with the living nightmare she experienced every time she heard it spoken to her during her childhood. It makes sense now, doesn't it? Mary's tearful emotions are stirred to their depths when she hears the words that caused her heart to tremble and faint when she was little.

When someone is rejected and as a result feels hurt, the mind looks for a way to avoid or deflect the pain. This is what a rejection habit is for, this is what a rejection habit is—a pain killer!

I can testify to the truth of how this works. I remember years ago staying somewhere with one of my friends for a few months. Though most of my stay was enjoyable, my experience in some things was very bitter. The mind-frying mental stress that I experienced was at times nearly unbearable. I came to look at that place as a hell without fire, and it was while staying there that I determined I never wanted to live in a hell if it didn't have flames with which to consume me. When I finally left that place, it was like a wonderful vacation, a very sweet dream. Though it was my plan to never return to that little mental hell on earth, due to the circumstances of life, hesitantly I returned.

As I approached the despised place while I was on my way there, I pressed myself against the back of the seat as if to avoid getting there sooner. As I went up the driveway, I started panicking with fearful forebodings. I began crying. The pain I had experienced at this place was too much for me. I had not yet experienced any pain, having just arrived, but that place was associated with a living hell, and I couldn't stand it. I seemed to be afraid of that place, though the place itself had never hurt me.

So it was in Mary's case. Andrew had never abused his wife or brought her pain or grief. However, unknowingly, he flipped the switch that turned on the lights of hell for his wife every time he said her full name. Thankfully, ever since their little discussion that one evening, Mary has been able to stop panicking whenever her husband says her name. One may wonder why Mary didn't go berserk when other people said her full name. Well, the thing is, she did, but only when with her close friends in whose presence she felt comfortable and safe, would she let loose her emotions that were going wild inside her. This is why she generally only went crazy when her husband said her full name and not when other people did.

Tim

"Tim! Why do you always look the other way when I am talking to you? Look me in the face!"

Tim turned his head thirty-five degrees to the right and gazed into his friend's eyes. "I don't know," he answered. "It's just a habit I have that I can't seem to get over." Had Tim known the reason why he habitually would not look at someone while conversing with them, he would have had an easier time getting over this habit, which often irritated his friends.

When Tim was a child, he began developing this habit. When he got into trouble for some reason, his mother or father would become infuriated with him, and the burning brimstone look on their faces often proved too painful for him to look at. So, in order to avoid the pain, he simply looked away. Because it is never a pleasant thing to look at someone's face when it is somehow dissatisfied with you, Tim would look in a different direction than that of his parents faces even when they were merely displeased with him. Tim also turned away when he saw his friend's irritated, disgusted, or disagreeing looks at him. He also avoided the faces of those whom he felt were always watching him to find some way in which they might criticize him.

Resorting to rejection habits to avoid emotional pain is kind of like taking Advil to kill headache pain instead of taking care of the reason you have the headache.

Eventually it became most comfortable to simply never look someone in the face while conversing, except for a quick glance now and again, or when he felt really comfortable with them to where he knew that unhappy looks and judgmental thoughts would not beam from their faces. At this point it was nearly unheard of for him to look somebody in the face at all if he was talking with them.

Tim's habit caused him much trouble with his family, friends, and coworkers. They were always fussing at him.. "Look me in the face when I am speaking to you." Little did they know that their fussing was only confirming his seeming inattention. Tim lost some of his friends due to his unexplainable habit. "If this guy is just going to ignore me," they each reasoned, "then I'll save my breath for someone who cares. Poo on him."

As a result of Tim's rejection, he unconsciously formed a habit that at the present moment of converse made him feel less pain but in the end only brought him more.

This is how all rejection habits are formed, the weird, and the simply disagreeable. When someone is rejected and as a result feels hurt, the mind looks for a way to avoid or deflect the pain. This is what a rejection habit is for, this is what a rejection habit is—a pain killer! These habits take care of the symptom but do not treat the real problem. Resorting to rejection habits to avoid emotional pain is kind of like taking Advil to kill headache pain instead of taking care of the reason you have the headache (lack of water, lack of fresh air, too much stress, etc).

Luke

"Luke! What do you think you are doing in the kitchen?" his father scolded.

"Looking for something to eat," he answered. "I'm hungry."

"Well you don't need to be eating right now," he barked. "Get out of the kitchen!"

Luke darted out of the room. This sort of thing was always happening to him. Whether he was looking for food to eat, getting it ready to eat, or eating the food itself, his father always seemed to be there fussing at him. If the problem wasn't what he was eating, then it was how or when he was eating it. This happened so often and so much that Luke came to a point where he felt uncomfortable and somewhat guilty if he found himself searching for or actually consuming food, unless he was sure his father would not notice him. He was always on edge when he ate at the table for fear his father would walk in the room, see him, and start verbally whipping him.

I'm sure you can guess what Luke's rejection habit became. He either hid every time he ate, hid the fact that he was eating at all, or simply didn't eat until he felt it was safe. Now, instead of eating at the dining room table, you would find him eating on the back porch, in his room, or standing by the kitchen door so that he could instantly vanish at the first sound of approaching footsteps.

It's not like Luke was getting in trouble for eating junk food and desserts all the time. Luke tried to be very health conscious and avoid eating anything he knew was unhealthy. And it wasn't like he ate up all the good and healthy food either. Often the good food his father had purchased would go bad because nobody ate it. And don't think that Luke was getting fussed at because he was constantly snacking either. Luke refused to snack because of the damaging effects he knew snacking had on the body. When he did eat, it was exactly on time. He became known around the house as the clock-watcher, for as soon as the kitchen stove's digital clock changed from 11:59 a.m. to 12:00 p.m., he would start looking for something tasty upon which to smack his lips.

Luke loved to eat. Too bad, however, that his father often spoiled his innocent enjoyment with his fretfulness. Luke's rejection habit would not have proved to be so troublesome to him if it wasn't strengthened by his friends' constant criticism concerning his eating habits. But they did not criticize him because they liked to find fault in him and point them out. In fact, they disliked doing this very much because they knew that Luke felt bad when they did. They made their remarks and comments for the purpose of trying to help him, because they thought he was making a great mistake in his diet, which would result in the premature death of their friend. Though Luke did believe 100 percent that this was the motive behind their sharp words, his belief system had already been molded and titled "Rejected," and so, even though the thought entered his mind, he never *really believed* they said these things because they accepted him. He *felt* rejection from them, so his rejection habit became stronger.

Luke's experiences over time proved to him to be so sour that he eventually didn't feel comfortable eating in the presence of hardly anyone, and so he would search for some way to get away from everyone while he was eating. Whether he did this by eating standing up on the other side of the vending machine where he was out of site of the break room's entrance at work, or whether he grabbed his food and ate it out in the car in front of his own home, he found some way he could eat in mental peace and serenity without constant anxiety and fear that someone would notice him and make some audible or silent comment about him or his food.

His friends thought he was "out to lunch" both literally and figuratively every time they noticed him hiding from them at mealtime. They didn't understand why Luke acted this way, and eventually they thought it was because he simply didn't want to be around them. Luke ended up feeling the tremors of these vibes as his friends began removing their attention from him. But what could Luke do? What could he do to get himself out of the pit of ruin into which he had been plunged and had plunged himself into? Either he eats in constant fear, or he loses his friends. What can one expect him to do?

Laura

"Laura! Would you stop running your mouth! Can't you see I'm trying to focus?!"

Laura was like any other eleven-year-old girl whose life is bubbling with excitement. She was learning many new things about life, her friends, and the world she lived in, and when she got excited about something, she loved to talk about it. Yet despite her desire to share her newfound knowledge with others, she often found that others just didn't want to hear what she had to say.

When Laura was younger, just like nearly all children, she sang her childish songs, talked her little girl chit chat to herself, and ran around and around the house making noise and banging on things. But her mother, who easily got irritated and was quite impatient and cranky at times, was always telling her to "Shut up!" "Be quiet!" "Either close your mouth or I'll close it for you." "If you don't stop screaming, then I'll give you something to scream about."

The scary thing is that her mother would do it. If Laura did not close her mouth, then her mother would tightly jerk duct tape around her daughter's head several times, securely sealing her lips. This would keep her quiet for hours as, silent and full of tears, she sat on her bed trying to painlessly pull the tape out of her hair and off her face. And if Laura did not stop screaming, then her mother would lay some thirty or forty jellyfish-like stinging stripes on her legs with a fine-tuned mahogany switch. Did Laura need to obey her mother? Of course! But did her mother use the right methods to teach Laura obedience as she, in her uncontrollable rage, wildly abused her daughter? No. But this is not a book on child rearing, so let's get back to the point.

Though Laura suffered all this as a child, these things alone did not turn her into the quiet, silent girl she later became. Her childish spirit was not yet broken; neither had her endurance yet waxed cold and brittle. However, her childhood experience laid the foundation for what was to make her teenage life a lonely one.

Some of Laura's hardest times in life were her teenage years from thirteen through sixteen when she found that her tongue was always seeming to get her in trouble. Her friends often scolded her, "Now why did you have to go and say that?!" "Don't you think before you run your yap?" "Can't you ever keep your mouth shut?"

Laura was often distraught. She did not purposefully say the wrong thing at the wrong time, but everything always *seemed* to come out that way. If it wasn't because of what she said or when she said it, then it was the mere fact that she said anything that caused her problems.

To fix her problems, Laura first tried to be very cautious about what she said and whose presence she said it in, taking into account all the circumstances of the present situation. When she found that this wasn't working, either because of a lack of knowledge or unwise decisions on her part, then she tried to simply cut back on what she had to say. This, she found, did help her some, even though she was not completely satisfied with the end results. Over time Laura became wiser and more thoughtful concerning what she had to say and how to say it. This helped her a lot, and she was now able to speak more freely. But still, several times a week, she found herself deeply regretting having opened her mouth and loosed her tongue.

Life was the most unforgiving toward Laura during her sixteenth and seventeenth years. In these years *it seemed to her* that, if she said anything, she would either be, corrected, criticized, argued with, ignored, scolded, or made to feel as if what she said wasn't important enough to be mentioned or talked about. Along with these troubles came the regret of saying things to individuals that she didn't want the world to know about. Whenever she did say these things, she often found that she might as well have posted them on the Internet or printed them in the newspaper. This led her to become distrustful of others, which somewhat separated her from them. But the worst of things was when Laura found out that one of her friends had been hurt by something she said. Laura loved her friends, and when she found out that something she had said had wounded one of them, in bitter tears for their pain, she unmercifully scolded herself and then tried earnestly to heal the wound she had made.

All of these things—the criticism, the arguments, the silence, the change of subjects, the rebukes, the gossip, the no longer secrets, the pain she caused, and ultimately the rejection that hit her, all coming from herself, her family, and her friends—gave her a mental disease that was not to be easily cured. "Why does everything I say always backfire on me?" she cried to herself. "Why does everything I say always end up either hurting me, or worse, those I love?"

One day, after hurting her best friend by accidentally ruining a surprise that her friend had planned for someone, Laura had had enough. She finally broke. As far as she was concerned, she had experienced and witnessed too much controversy, grief, and pain as the result of her speaking.

> *It's almost as if you cherish your rejection habits. It's as if you enjoy being absolutely miserable...*

Rejection had engrained into her mind that if she opened her mouth, someone would be wounded as a result. Therefore, she said nothing but the bare necessities, and even these she often cut short. She became known as the silent girl who sat by herself away from everyone and who said absolutely nothing to anyone. She was a freak, a weirdo.

Her friends didn't understand her new behavior or the reason for it. They condemned her as selfish and hardheaded. Little did they know that it was out of blind love for them that she had made her decision to refuse to speak. This caused alienation between them. Blind love it was that did this, but love none the less. And oh how Laura suffered in separation from her only joy in life, her friends! Oh the brokenness of spirit she experienced as if a freshly tempered, double-edged dagger had penetrated her heart and was slowly making its way through! In silence she wept in her grief, and none of her friends knew it.

Ruth

Ruth's experience was similar to Mark's. Without going into the horrible specifics, Ruth was always being mistreated by her friends. They were constantly found criticizing, deserting, mocking, using, misusing, abusing, and gossiping about her. Ruth strived to be patient with her abusive friends. She loved them and let them abuse her for years before she finally broke from the pain of it. At this point, she left her friends to themselves and no longer had anything to do with them. "If this is what friends do to each other," she said to herself, "then I don't want any!" And so she chose to be friendless.

This choice ruined her. Her human need and desire for friendship, without being filled, drained her spirit. But even today she still chooses to not let anyone into her life. Is it unreasonable for Ruth to do this? Isn't she out of her mind? Isn't she being ridiculous and unreasonable? With an attitude like that, doesn't she deserve to be friendless? Many of us would say yes, but we don't see things through Ruth's eyes. We don't answer these questions with a thorough knowledge of her experience in mind.

Doing the Things You Hate

Often you may find yourself dying to get out of your rejection habits so that you can be closer to your friends and so that you can live the life you are longing for. Unfortunately, you probably find it nearly impossible to break these habitual chains. You find that they are ruling your life as if you were merely a puppet. It's almost as if you cherish your rejection habits. It's as if you enjoy being absolutely miserable. On the contrary, you are simply a slave of rejection and the habits that it has formed in you. But there is hope. Just hang on!

Not everyone who suffers the results of rejection will realize it. For too long I couldn't understand why I seemed to love being so miserable and separated from those people who meant the most to me. This was a mystery I could not fathom. I was bound in the chains of ignorance and torture, which seemed to me as strong as some enchanting spell of overmastering witchcraft. My only explanation for my seeming love of absolute misery was that I had a mental problem. I was dying to spend time with those I loved so much. But instead of doing so, I rejected and hurt them, and myself. Oh how strong the power of rejection is! Oh how mysterious, and oh how wicked!

Better Vision

Let me ask you, do you now understand Ruth's refusal to accept friends into her life after years of being burglarized by them? Do you think Ruth is out of her mind? Do you think she is being ridiculous and unreasonable? On the contrary! Ruth is being very reasonable. In fact, Ruth has been doing all of the reasoning. She has reasoned from cause to effect, and in her eyes she has made a wise decision, while we, instead of reasoning at all, simply judge her and proclaim her irrational, ridiculous, and unreasonable. But we are the irrational and unreasonable ones, not her. Though her reasoning may not help her through life, at least she has done it, while we have only judged her and proved ourselves deserving of receiving the very treatment we have given to her.

Though her reasoning may not help her through life, at least she has done it...

Oh how thoughtless it is for us to judge each other by outward appearances when we are clueless as to why people do what they do and ignorant of what the rejection process has done to them. What did this process do to Jim? It caused him to refuse help, gifts, and love from others. "Oh how rude, thoughtless, unreasonable, and unthankful," we say. "If he is going to act like that then he doesn't deserve anything offered to him." Are you judging him? Did he not suffer enough, or does he need your critical and unmerciful judgment as well?

What did this process do to Rachel? It caused her to spend hours in the bathroom primping. But we, shortsighted critics, only thoughtlessly say to her, "Oh, you are such an extremist! A fanatic! You waste so much time!"

What about Rose? She suffered severe foot pain because of her actions that sprang from feelings of rejection. Are you going to add to her suffering by saying within her hearing, "I can't believe she is so stupid! She deserves those flat feet."

How about Joe? "What! He doesn't even want his wife helping him in the kitchen?! What a way to treat her when she just wants to help. What a jerk!" we say in disgust. Did not Joe suffer enough? Must we add to it?

And how do we view our dear Sapphire who is contemplating suicide? She was made to feel as if every problem, sadness, disappointment, and pain that others suffered from was her fault. "I can't believe that such a beautiful and talented girl with such a nice life and so many friends would be so stupid as to want to kill herself. What an idiot?" we say. Have you walked in her shoes? Have you lived her life? Have you viewed the world with the crippling glasses of rejection that she has? *Then leave her alone!*

If people don't act according to what we think they should, we either consider them weird or as having a problem. But are they? Do they? It is highly probable that they are neither weird nor have a problem. In fact, they are probably perfectly normal considering those unknown facts of their lives that we never see or take into account. Perhaps we are the ones who have a problem. Our problem is that we like to act as an evil god-master and pronounce judgment on them. How cruel of us! All we accomplish for those poor rejected ones by our judgment is cause them to feel more of the rejection that has helped to make them who they are. This will cause them to continue to act the same way, so that we can once again judge them, so that they can feel more rejected. What a wicked, subtle cycle we have set up to destroy us all and increase the suffering in this world.

The victims of rejection often come to a point in which they don't care anymore. They don't care about themselves or what happens to them in life. This is deep self-rejection. But it must be clear that *it's not that they don't care, they do!* But if perhaps they didn't care, wouldn't that help to kill the pain of rejection? Yes. And this is why some people go so far with rejection that they choose not to hope anymore.

Hope and care have become their enemy, because in their mind, every time they hoped and cared, the hope was disappointed and the care increased the pain of rejection. To hope and care is what they really want, but they can't stand the thought of hoping and caring because hope and care have become identified with pain. They don't want to hope and care, and therefore, they shove those thoughts away. And yet they can't shove them away completely because other people care about them and they know that not hoping for or caring about anything in life will hurt those who love them. This they cannot afford to do. They cannot stand to hurt those they love, and yet they cannot stand to hope and care anymore. They are stuck in a nightmare from which they cannot escape. Or can they?

But if perhaps they didn't care, wouldn't that help to kill the pain of rejection?...

So congratulations! You don't have a "mental illness." In fact, you're normal considering what you've experienced in life. And no, you don't need to take psychotropic drugs to fix your problem. There is no scientific proof that shows that "mental illnesses" even exist, nothing to show that they are physically there. And if they aren't physically there, you cannot treat them with drugs. They've never proven that "mental illnesses" are the result of a chemical imbalance in the brain. This appears to be nothing more than a theory that has been adopted to make the psychiatric profession look scientific when there is nothing scientific about it at all.

No, your friend doesn't have bipolar disorder. Bipolar disorder is a name that the psychiatric world has given to people that have severe up's and down's. So the question is, is it a disorder? Is it an illness? Or is it *life*? True, if you stir people's brains around a little bit with highly dangerous drugs, it may seem like it helps them so long as they are on them. If you get drunk, it will do the same thing. Drugs don't restore anything, but re-educating your brain can actually fix the psychological problems you have. Yay!

The how-to-fix-the-problem information is coming, just hold on.

Chapter 4

Their Main Weapons

As has been made clear, the rejection process, with all of it woes, begins with *feelings* of rejection. It matters not how much love you have in your heart. If a person feels rejected by you, the terrible process will either be initiated or, as would be more likely, the rejection file will be updated to aid in warding off future emotional pain.

When dealing with others, there are certain things you do not do or say if you want them to feel accepted by you. Parents, when dealing with their children, often break every law of their child's mind, reject them in every possible way, and then expect their children to do what they say and feel that they love them. It is one of the most dumbfounding things a person can ever witness.

Threats, indifference, distrust, belittlement, criticism, and mind-reading must *not* be avoided in our dealing with each other, *they must be perfectly extinct!* All of these things will bring emotional discomfort to an individual, *guaranteed*. There is no escaping this. They will all be consciously or subconsciously detected by the mind as intruders. They are all violators of the emotional being, and everyone will feel, to some degree or another, violated by them. Some may not feel violated, but that is because they have been led into self-rejection where they have already violated themselves to keep you from doing it to them. They've inflicted the pain upon themselves so that you couldn't hurt them anymore.

Threats

Should someone threaten to kill you if you did not hand them your wallet, would you feel that this person really accepted and loved you unconditionally or would you feel alarmed, intruded upon, and violated because you are about to be either robbed, murdered, or both? The feelings lean the same direction with all

> *Defending oneself does not consist in surrendering... To defend oneself from an attack means to resist the attack. Key word—resist.*

levels of threats. Whether it is a threat to take away your life or a threat to take away your candy bar, all genuine threats cause the one threatened to feel emotional discomfort.

How many times, in trying to discipline their children, have you seen parents threaten their child into obedience? And to what avail? When the emotional being is attacked, it is only natural for us to defend ourselves. Defending oneself does not consist in surrendering the will over to that which the conscious or subconscious mind has detected and identified as an enemy. To defend oneself from an attack means to *resist* the attack. Key word—*resist*.

If someone threatened to kill you if you didn't give him your money, you would either try to resist the criminal or surrender your money to him, hoping that your life would be spared. The supreme desire obviously would be to somehow resist the thief and save both your life and your money. But either choice you make, you would still feel violated afterwards as long as you didn't die, and you would take future precautions to avoid being violated again in such an extreme way.

When someone is threatened, the threatened individual feels

alarmed and violated. His supreme desire is to resist the intruder and not lose anything in the threat. This is the goal, and the one threatened will gladly fight for whatever he can get.

Now, in disciplining their children, parents do not necessarily go so far as to threaten to take away their child's life, but they will threaten them in countless other ways. "Do this," a father says, "or you won't be able to go to your friend's house." "Do that," a mother says, "or I'll take away your cell phone." And to what avail?

> *By your threats, all you create in them is a desire to resist you.*

The true object of discipline is to train a child for proper self-government. It is to enlist his will and his reason on the side of what is right, just, and true. It is to inspire him to want to do what is right and choose to do it. It is to prepare him to stand for what is right and to do what is right, regardless of consequences and surrounding circumstances. Anything short of this fails to reach the mark of all true discipline.

Do you now see why threatening a child into doing right is falling short of the whole purpose of discipline? By your threats, all you create in them is a desire to *resist* you. By threatening them you have proven yourself to their conscious or subconscious mind as an enemy, a criminal who has violated them and must be warded off. Oh how many times have children been led into disregarding a parent's wise instruction, not because he was trying to resist the instruction itself, but because he was trying to resist the parent, which his mind has calculated as an unjust tyrant.

If you threaten a child, why should she want to do anything you say? I mean come on, *you threatened her!* By threatening her you have just inspired her to not want to do anything you tell her. In fact, when she might have done it before, since you threatened her and intruded upon her rights, she will not do it in effort to resist your tyranny. And is that not a just cause? No, it's not a just cause to resist mom and dad's wise instruction, but it is just to resist criminal usurpers.

Children, youth, young adults, and the aged all have reasoning capacities. A child can understand wise reasoning and counsel and be led to value, love, and follow it. But a child's mind sees no justice in threats that are a violation of his rights. He may not understand the terminology of it all, and he may not even understand why he feels violated, but his built-in defense mechanism identifies threats as unjust intruders that must be resisted. If you are the one who threatens him, you become identified with that

If you are the one who threatens him, you become identified with that threat, and you must be resisted. Threaten a child into doing what is right, and you will be resisted.

threat, and you must be resisted. Threaten a child into doing what is right, and you will be resisted. Even if he does surrender and in the end does what you requested, his mind is calculating (consciously or subconsciously) a way to resist you in the future. He is not led to see and value the justice of doing what is right because the threat gets all the attention.

Once a person has become more than temporarily identified with emotional discomfort in someone's mind, it is extremely difficult for that person to lose that identity in the other person's mind. However, this identity must be lost if they ever hope to become identified with acceptance and become the victim's friend. Stop rejecting them, don't violate the laws of their mind, only do that which will make them feel accepted, and the rejection identity will be lost.

Threatening a child into right doing or bribing her into it will not result in the goal of true discipline. Threats and bribes cause the child to do right because of circumstances. It does not train her to proper self-government. It does not fit her to stand for the right and to do it regardless of the consequences. All that it might accomplish is get a one-time only selfish response because it appeals to the child's immediate comfort and wants. Foster a child's selfishness, and it will grow. She will end up a self-centered individual who is nothing more than a curse to the human race.

When you threaten children into doing what is right, they are not led to reason out the justice of why they should do right. All they can think about is that if they don't do what they are told, they will suffer. Do you see how this only appeals to fear and the individual's immediate comfort? It does not appeal to reason, and therefore, they will not be led to reason. And then, when they prove themselves disobedient, we jump on their case for not being reasonable. Well whose fault is that? Did you appeal to their sense of reason and justice, or did you appeal to and play upon their fears?

If they are being unreasonable, it's because you were unreasonable *first*. You were the one that didn't reason with them. The child might have reasoned with you had you appealed to his reason, but you appealed to his fears. You resorted to disrespect to gain his loyalty, and you only gained his disrespect in return. Although you disrespected him first, should he disrespect you? No, he shouldn't. But you have not taught him to do what is right because it is right; you have taught him to do what is right or else he will be punished. You've messed it up for yourself, and you have no one to blame but yourself.

As is now obvious, threatening someone into doing something is not an effective way of getting people to do what is right or to make them feel accepted by you. Unless your goal is to ruin someone by making them feel bad or to arouse in them a spirit of fear and/or resistance, threats will not accomplish your purpose. They can accomplish nothing for good because they are evil. Just as darkness cannot possibly produce light no matter how hard it tries, even so, doing evil cannot produce good results no matter how much effort and reasoning is put behind it.

But don't forget the difference between a threat and a warning. A threat is the spirit of "do this or else." But the character of a warning is "because I love you, I want to inform you of the consequences." The threat triggers a false motive for obedience, but the warning appeals to reason and a spirit of love.

Indifference

"Mom! Tell Eddie to get out of my room. He's in here annoying me," Sarah yells.

"I've already told him to get out of there. If he doesn't leave, then just ignore him."

"Mom! Sarah took my bouncy-ball. Tell her to give it back," Eddie complains.

"I don't care if she took your bouncy-ball. I told you to stay out of her room. Get out of there right now!"

How is the daughter supposed to feel like Mommy cares about her when Mommy just blew her off and told her to just deal with her brother's annoyances? How is the son supposed to feel like Mommy cares about him and what brings him joy in life when she just said, "I don't care." Going completely off of what his mother said, the child determines that his mom doesn't care that his sister took his bouncy-ball. While he may have been at fault for being in his sister's room, his rights have been violated now as well. If mommy won't defend and fight for his rights, then he must do it himself. No one cares about him, and so if he is going to survive, he's got to be the one to do the fighting.

"Mom! Eddie is still in my room and now he's hitting me. Make him stop!" Sarah screams.

> *Everyone needs to feel accepted, and if you don't make them feel that you accept them when they can see that you have ample opportunity to do so, they will feel like you reject them.*

Stomp! Stomp! Stomp! Mother bangs down the hall toward Sarah's room, opens the door, and screams, "Eddie, I told you to get out of Sarah's room! Get out right now! Go to your room and don't come out or I'll whip your little butt!"

"But Mom, she stole my bouncy-ball!" he says as he slowly heads toward his room.

"I told you I don't care if she stole your stupid ball!" she yells as she slaps her son square in the mouth. Eddie screams at his mom for being mean and then runs off to his room crying and utterly furious. Mom then turns to her daughter. "Why did you take his stupid ball?!"

"Because he came in my room and started annoying me and you didn't do anything about it because you were too involved on the computer," Sarah replies.

The mother then slaps her daughter in the face as she yells, "Don't you talk back to me you disrespectful child! There, maybe that will teach you for talking back to your mother."

Very sadly, this seems to be a highly common occurrence in many homes. Children are disrespectful to their parents and parents to their children, and much of it is because the parents cause their children emotional discomfort. Careless indifference was the issue in the above incidence. When Sarah sought her mother's help, her mother didn't seem to care enough about her daughter to defend her rights in requiring her brother to respect her privacy. The daughter reasons that since Mom doesn't care enough about her to defend her rights, she will take action to defend her rights herself. She then violates her brother's rights by taking away his bouncy-ball in an effort to get him to leave her room.

Once again there is a need and a cry for their mother's help, and once again there is manifest indifference. Then hell breaks loose. Was it necessary? No. Mother could have took care of the situation before it worsened, and she could have controlled herself far better than she did. But her seeming indifference ended up causing great problems.

Let us say that you go to your spouse one evening and tell him about how you were mistreated earlier that day. What would you do should he respond by saying, "You know, honey, I don't really care." Would not this be a direct attack at your emotional being? The person that you've chosen to love, cherish, and spend your whole life with has told you he doesn't care about your pain. This itself is painful. It is emotionally destructive. You've been totally rejected, and how are you supposed to respond to it?

The rejection process has already been initiated in the past, and this is just another file update that will be analyzed and used as important information that will give you the tools to keep him from hurting you like this again. And what course of action do you think your brain would calculate and take to keep you out of pain? A likely course would be that you no longer tell your spouse when you are hurt. And that's the perfect way to ruin a relationship.

Now, going back to the family blowup. Mother's indifference made it very difficult for her children to do what was right because they were both violated and no one was there to do anything about it but themselves. They made a mess of the situation and then used facts and screaming to defend themselves against their mother's indifferent rage.

The daughter defended herself by pointing out that the problem was mostly her mother's fault while the son screamed at his mother for it. His mother wasn't there to defend his rights, and when he tried to stick up for himself, he got slapped for it. He really doesn't feel hurt because his mother doesn't seem to care about him. He's learned to expect that, and so he rejects himself and doesn't feel much pain at all.

After slapping her daughter, Mother had said to her, "There, maybe that will teach you for talking back to your mother." But what exactly did it teach her? What did this whole incident teach both of the children? It only confirmed the old half-conscious conclusion that Mother doesn't always care enough about their problems to help them out when they are in a hard spot. It's taught them that if they need help asking their mother for it might only make matters worse, because she won't necessarily do anything about it unless she comes to the point of getting mad. Therefore, they should do something about it themselves. Yes, they'll probably get in trouble for it in the end, but what else can they do? Sarah is annoyed and Eddie has his ball stolen—what do you expect them to do?

Not showing someone that you care about them when you have a good opportunity to do so is to reject them. You don't have to do something mean to someone to hurt them emotionally. All you have to do is not do something nice. Everyone needs to feel accepted, and if you don't make them feel that you accept them when they can see that you have ample opportunity to do so, they will feel like you reject them. Ignoring people, being indifferent to their wants and needs, all prove as evidence to them that you don't really care. Not being kind and caring toward someone will just as much start the rejection process in them as will backstabbing them directly.

Distrust

When people manifest confidence in you, how does it make you feel? For the average individual, when someone has confidence in them, it gives them a sense of acceptance. They feel trusted as they see that others are depending upon their integrity and faithfulness. It gives them a sense of honor, which itself has ennobling effects.

They feel like they are valued as respectable individuals who are worthy of trust and responsibility, and it gives them an inward sense of dignity.

Consequential punishment should never be given or pointed to as a motive to get a person to change...

On the other hand, when someone manifests distrust toward another, they feel disappointed as they see that others look upon them with suspicion and judge them as incapable and dishonest. The value they place upon themselves decreases as they see others value them on such a low level. They lose their sense of dignity and the effects often prove demoralizing. Since they are not looked upon and treated as respectable and worthy individuals, they feel no need to try to live up to the title and are satisfied with accepting a low self-esteem.

Trust is one of those topics that can be a very sticky one. You can't just trust everyone with everything; wisdom must bear rule in order to prevent disaster. Here, however, we will discuss the common, everyday trust between family and friends. The kind of trust that believes your daughter when she says she got all her homework done and that trusts

75

your friend to mail a package on time so that your brother in Florida receives his present by his birthday.

Suppose your spouse has lied to you a few times during your marriage and it has become difficult for you to trust them. Should you question their every word and ask them constantly whether or not they are lying to you, you will utterly destroy your relationship. They will feel like garbage because their own life partner doesn't trust them. They will recognize that you don't really trust anything they say. As a natural result of the rejection process, when you ask them a question, they will have little to no desire to answer it, reasoning within themselves that you won't believe them anyway and that there is therefore no point in wasting their breath only to be hurt again when you manifest your unbelief in their word. Thus, alienation *will* result. No, they shouldn't have lied to you, but that doesn't mean you should hurt them with your distrust, which is calculated to break them down and destroy them.

But will bringing up the past mistakes of others make the present situation any better?

Distrust is the result of rejection. Children who are very young, who have not yet suffered the rejection that comes from being tricked and lied to, will naturally trust nearly anyone and everyone until they are violated. Suppose you are trying to get a two year old to take a spoonful of oatmeal. The two year old doesn't like the oatmeal, and when you try to feed it to her, she seals her lips and turns her head away. Let's say you now offer her a bite of smashed banana or something she likes, and upon her obvious acceptance of it with a wide-open mouth, should you quickly switch spoons and sneak oatmeal into her mouth, she will feel tricked and violated. You were deceitful with her, and you've just knocked over the first domino and set her up for a life of suspicion and distrust. Why should she trust you now? Others? Maybe. But you? No way!

If someone lies to you, you will feel disrespected and violated, like your personal rights were intruded upon, and the rejection process will create in you a spirit of distrust for the purpose of keeping you safe from being violated again. It's only natural, but here nature hurts, not only you, but those you love.

If someone has proven to you that they cannot be trusted, it will never suffice to simply not trust them anymore. This will help neither you nor them. Through calm reasoning and patient love, they need to understand the reason that you do not trust them is not because you don't want to but because they've proven it unwise for you to trust them. They need to see that you want to trust them but that the reason you cannot is because they have not chosen to change. They must be given ample opportunity to change. Then, if no change has been made, you can kindly explain to them that you cannot trust them, not in an effort to get them to be honest with you, but because *they will not* be honest with you.

This is how all punishments should be enforced. Consequential punishment should never be given or pointed to as a motive to get a person to change, but it should be explained to them that the reason they will be punished is because they have proven *they will not change*. To set up punishment as a motive for right doing will never give anyone a lasting reason to do what is right. Once the punishment is removed, they will go back to their foolish ways because their reason for doing right was taken away. The same holds true with bribery. Remove the reward for right-doing, and they will no longer do right.

Criticism and Humiliation

Have you ever been put on the spot? You know, like that moment when you felt all eyes suddenly focus on you immediately after they discovered something about you that was rather embarrassing. Other than embarrassed, as that is obvious, how did you feel? How much did it affect your day, your week, or even your whole life? Do you even know? And what about that horrible time when someone brought to your remembrance that really stupid mistake you made? The worst part about it was not that they reminded you but rather that it was spoken within the reach of other curious ears. Correct?

Her father did not realize it, but in the moment when his daughter needed him the most, he belittled her pain. The belittlement was by comparison.

To put someone on the spot, to make them feel that all attentive minds are criticizing and judging their every thought and motive, is just plain wicked. No one should be made to feel that they are under the unmerciful inspection of another human being. The effects of such evils are calculated only to destroy. Think now for a minute and determine in your mind what the rejection process could do to another should they be placed under such withering influences.

Often, people remind others about how they messed up in the past. They think that somehow reminding them of their past mistakes will help them understand why they can't be trusted, why they cannot have this or that privilege, or why they need to change. But will bringing up the past mistakes of others make the present situation any better? It could, but it depends upon the manner in which it is brought up. However, for the most part, as is commonly witnessed in human

78

interactions, bringing up old dirt will never help to get the floor clean. Forget the past. Statistics prove nothing about the future.

Belittlement

People belittle each other's pain and experience all the time without meaning to hurt anyone. They often are just trying to help one who is hurt, but they can end up hurting them even more if they are not careful. And even if they are careful, since it only matters if someone feels hurt, you can hurt someone no matter how careful you are.

"Daddy!" Sarah sobbed as she ran toward her father. "My best friend said that she hates me and that we are not friends anymore."

"Aww! I'm sorry, honey! Now, now, stop crying," her father sympathized. "My best friend did the same thing to me when I was only thirteen years old, but you are fifteen now."

Her father did not realize it, but in the moment when his daughter needed him the most, he belittled her pain. The belittlement was by comparison. All her father wanted to do was show his daughter that he understood her pain, that he was there for her, and help her to stop crying and cheer up. But he sought to do this in a way that made light of her pain. She was perhaps too emotionally distraught to consciously recognize the belittlement, but her subconscious caught it.

Telling someone what they think or what they will do is a violation of his personal rights, and therefore, he will feel under attack.

People compare their life experiences with each other all the time, and when the opportunity presents itself, they often show how they had it harder than the other person. It gives them a sense of pride, a sense of, "Well, I've had it harder than you have, and I handled it better than you are handling your easier experience; therefore, I am better than you are." This belittlement, if not recognized and properly dealt with, will cause one to look upon himself as less perhaps than he really is. The value that he places on himself will be lowered in his mind because he just doesn't reach the level of Joe who had it harder than himself. The effects of this are obvious.

To help someone who is in pain, it is better not to do it by comparison. Just tell the injured one that you understand. Tell them how well they are handling the situation, and do everything to lift them up. Comparing them with yourself should only be done if it belittles you. Not because it belittles you, but because the natural result of belittling yourself raises them up in their mind. When someone is feeling down, be careful not to bury them deeper. Say and do that which will bring them up out of the pit they are in and set them on their feet once again, braced, and ready to face the world.

Mind Reading

Studying the statistical history of a certain individual's actions and responses does not determine what they will do in the future. Statistics prove nothing about the future.

This is one of those nasty little creatures that all of us have probably bit someone with. The human mind stores information, thinks, reasons, and chooses, all inside of a highly private box. The only way that information can be gathered from it is if it so chooses to release it. But some people seem as if they would deny this fact.

Have you ever said anything similar to the following phrases: "Oh, I know what you were thinking. You were thinking such and such."

"But I know what you're going to do. You are going to do such and such." If you have ever said anything like this to another person, I have a question for you. How did you know? Perhaps you have very good reasons to be able to somewhat predict what someone would think or do. Perhaps you've studied them and watched them through the years to where you know how they will respond and what they will think to nearly everything. This is a good achievement, but it cannot be used as your right to tell someone what they think or what they will do.

What goes on inside someone's mind is his right to know and keep to himself. No other human being has the right to expose that information contrary to the wishes of that person. Telling someone what they think or what they will do is a violation of his personal rights, and therefore, he will feel under attack. And often the mind reader knows nothing of what he is talking about.

Studying the statistical history of a certain individual's actions and responses does not determine what they will do in the future. Statistics *prove nothing* about the future; they can only prove certain things concerning certain circumstances in the past. An individual can change if they so choose. But when we go and tell them what they think and what they will do, we are telling them that who they are is who they will forever be. They will never grow and develop, and whatever low level they were upon, they will remain upon because that is what statistics prove. Should someone tell you that you are a liar and always will be because that is what your past history proves, it is not necessary to ask how that would make you feel.

But let us suppose that you were right in your conclusion of what someone thought or would do. What good would it do to tell it to them? Would it do good at all? If you tell someone what they think or will do, you are exposing private information that is not your right to distribute. Even though you may only be telling the person whose mind

81

you think you are reading, you are violating them. You are assuming information about them that you cannot possibly know as a matter of fact, and it is this that makes them feel violated. To assume something about another's character that you cannot possibly know for certain is treading on forbidden ground. Don't do it!

Conclusion

There are many other things that must be avoided to help keep others from feeling rejected by you. The purpose of this book is not to give you a list of do's and don'ts to memorize, rather it is to give you the general principles for you to inculcate into your interactions with others. The don'ts are more of a matter of common sense. One doesn't need to be told that humiliating someone, putting them on the spot, yelling at them, and stomping on their foot will make them feel rejected; it's a matter of reality. The above don'ts that were given were expounded upon because they are the major forms of rejection that are commonly accepted as somewhat okay things to do, or at least, normal things that are commonly done.

> *Instead of giving someone a command, make a request. It will give them a greater sense of liberty. They will feel freer to open up as they see that they aren't pressured to defend themselves.*

When interacting with others, instead of having a memorized list of things not to do, it is far more effective and easier to remember the principle that is behind all of the don'ts. Whatever you say or do must not make the other person feel emotional discomfort, but rather it should be calculated to make them feel more emotionally comfortable than they already are. They should be made to feel more liberated. Instead of giving someone a command, make a request. It will give them a greater sense of liberty. They will feel freer to open up as they see that they aren't pressured to defend themselves. But if you say and do things that put them in a defensive mode, you're setting them up to be ruined.

Everyone has the right to be treated with kindness. They own that right just as much as they own the right to eat food, drink water, and breath air. If someone starves you, they are stealing your right to eat food. If someone is mean to you, they are stealing your right to be treated kindly. Belittling someone, threatening them, or being indifferent to their wants and needs is just as much stealing from them as is shoplifting. It doesn't matter how much they stole from you first; if you steal from them, you are a criminal and should be put behind bars. You broke the law just as much as they did, and no amount of self-justifying excuses or "reasons" will get you out of jail. End of story.

If someone starves you, they are stealing your right to eat food. If someone is mean to you, they are stealing your right to be treated kindly. Belittling someone, threatening them, or being indifferent to their wants and needs is just as much stealing from them as is shoplifting.

Chapter 5

Our Main Defenses

Defending Ourselves

The best defense against rejection is no defense at all. Self-rejection and all the rejection habits that form as the natural result of being rejected are developed because of the mind's built-in defense mechanism. No defense is literally your only defense against feelings of rejection. Instead of "stuffing it," let the feelings of rejection pay their toll on you. If you try to defend yourself against emotional pain, you will end up rejecting yourself or will develop some nasty rejection habit, both of which will make your interactions with others more difficult. Thus, many have been led to miserably hate their lives.

The best way to deal with emotional discomfort and pain is to literally let it stomp all over you. This may not be the best policy in a bull fight, but here it is the only key to victory. It is far better to let the pain hurt and the tears flow than to stuff all of your pain and fight back. Let the emotional pain of rejection swing around the pole and hit you like a ton of bricks. This is the only way to avoid larger problems in the future when all of the pain you stuffed inside you has poisoned your entire system and comes up out of its grave only to send you to it.

You must understand that it is impossible for you to experience acceptance unless you first risk being rejected!

It seems that most people

stuff their pain for years before they realize what doing so has done to them. This can make it extremely difficult when they are told that the only way for them to recover from rejection is to allow all of the pain they stuffed to finally beat them up.

By what authority does our past gain the right to dictate what our future will be? Shall our minds, which value so much the freedom that is rightfully ours, be the very thing that imprisons us in the darkest dungeons of an alternate reality?

As for letting down your defenses, when you bring them down, you will end up feeling the pain of rejection again. But that's fine. Let it hurt. It's all part of the plan. Stop rejecting yourself to avoid the pain, and stop trying to be someone you're not just to *feel* accepted when you're really not. If you want to overcome rejection and enjoy the freedom of true acceptance from others, you must understand that *it is impossible for you to experience acceptance unless you first risk being rejected!* You must first make yourself vulnerable and place yourself helplessly in someone else's hands in trembling trust before anyone can have the opportunity to accept you. Give them a chance, but more importantly, give yourself a chance—another chance.

Freedom

Nearly everyone in the world is a slave to someone or something. Whether to their master, family, friends, work, or habits, they are in bondage. They are manipulated into doing the very things they do not want to do. The worst type of servitude, however, is that given to rejection.

But the question is, what exactly is it that takes away our freedom and makes us the slaves of rejection? It is nothing more than our own mind. It seems that one of the most common ways that people give up their freedom is by thinking they don't have any.

People are controlled by their own minds against their own wishes. The rejection habits that have woven themselves into their characters, and the deep-seated self-rejection, poisoning the very springs of life, are what control their every action. But why should we allow what others have done to us to control us? By what authority does our past gain the right to dictate what our future will be? Shall our minds, which value so much the freedom that is rightfully ours, be the very thing that imprisons us in the darkest dungeons of an alternate reality? The human brain's defense mechanism can be good in its place, but once it asserts itself to the position of a tyrant, then *it is time for war!*

But the question is, what exactly is it that takes away our freedom and makes us the slaves of rejection? It is nothing more than *our own mind*. It seems that one of the most common ways that people give up their freedom is by thinking they don't have any. If you don't believe you have freedom, then you won't act like you are free. If a slave is freed from his master after years and years of service, but because it is "too good to be true" doesn't believe that he is really set free, then what do you think he will do? It's simple. He will keep on serving his master, not because he is still a slave and has no freedom, but because he is bound by the chains of his own mind, which declare him in bondage. In reality he is free, but because he doesn't accept the good news as true, he is just as surely a slave as if he really wasn't free. He is securely kept as a prisoner of his own mind.

You may be messed up in the head, which cannot be instantly fixed, but you can keep that mess from controlling your present life.

So when it comes to how to be liberated from our own minds, we first must ask if we are really in bondage. Are we? Since it is our minds that bind us to self-rejection and its habits, it must then be our minds that liberate us. Are you free? If you're not, then you can choose to be. With your mind you can make a conscious choice to be free from rejection. Right here and right now you can be liberated from what rejection has done to you. It is as simple as acknowledging that, since you have chosen to be free from rejection, *you are free.*

The difficulty arises when you have the choice to be free, but you don't *want* to be free. Rejection has proven itself to be your best friend. You enjoy rejection. It is your greatest pleasure to be perfectly miserable. After all, you're in control that way, and then you can know more or less what to expect. No one can hurt you because you're the boss. Fuss on everyone. Another question, is this who you want to be? Is this who you choose to be? Or is this who you *feel* you want to be?

You can't change your past experiences or the knowledge you've acquired from them. There is no delete button you can push to incinerate that rejection file with all of its painful feelings and conclusions. You can't just up and forget everything no matter how hard you try. But you can choose to not be controlled by your past; you can choose to not be controlled by rejection. You may be messed up in the head, which cannot be instantly fixed, but you can keep that mess from controlling your present life. Though it may be a mess, you are not forced to trip over the junk.

Somewhere inside, everyone desires freedom. This is why people choose to cling to rejection, because it sets them free from what other people can do to them. But it is not true freedom, because then you are in bondage to yourself. But why be in bondage to anyone, including yourself? Why be bound by an authority that makes you miserable? Will you be controlled by feelings? Shall pain be your master?

> *Somewhere inside, everyone desires freedom. This is why people choose to cling to rejection, because it sets them free from what other people can do to them.*

But do not stuff your feelings so you don't feel pain. Let the pain run you over like a semi-truck, just don't let it control you and alter your life. If you stuff your feelings, it only makes self-rejection all the harder to break.

There is, of course, the reasoning that if we reject ourselves and continue to live out rejection habits we'll just suffer and that's the end of it. But is that the end of it? Doesn't it affect others? It does. And when you reject yourself and act like you are rejected, others will feel rejected *by you*. And who are you to reject them? To trample upon their rights and drive them like a stake into their graves. If you cause someone who is already wired to self-destruct to feel emotional discomfort, are you going to be the cause of her meltdown? The only way you can live without helping to enslave others or being enslaved yourself is to feel the pain but *know* that you are free from rejection. Choose to be free. Doing this will set in motion a domino of impulses that will vibrate throughout the world and set other prisoners free.

Now is the time to assert the liberty that is rightfully yours, to send self-rejection a pink slip, and to live as a free human being. Be a freedom fighter and work to free others from the nightmare you've lived in. Break the chains of bondage and liberate the poor captives who cannot yet help themselves.

But when you seek to liberate others, you must do so without violating the rights of another human being. If you do this, you are defeating your whole mission. We cannot be selective in who we steal rights from and who we don't. That's hypocrisy. If you reject Bob at work because he hurt you first, but not his daughter Laura at home, the pain Bob felt will manifest itself upon Laura at home. We must be kind to all. Everyone has the right to be treated with kindness.

So go now. Kick rejection in the pants by being who you've wanted to be this whole time. Don't *try* to keep the laws of the human mind, *choose* to keep them. When tempted to break them, when evil thoughts flood your mind and evil feelings permeate your body, when every fiber of your being wants to explode and let someone have it, don't *try* to resist the temptation, *choose* to resist it. *Stick to that choice no matter what,* and victory is yours. *This is the key!* You are not controlled by thoughts and feelings that are against your will. Your power to choose is in control, and whatever you choose is what you will do. You are *not* your feelings; you are who you choose to be.

Now is the time to assert the liberty that is rightfully yours, to send self-rejection a pink slip, and to live as a free human being.

"He's right over there. Why don't you help him? Don't just sit there! Look at him! He's sitting on the edge of the street despising his own life. His head is bowed down in sorrow; his spirits are crushed.

You are not your feelings; you are who you choose to be.

He's sad and discouraged, and he sees no reason to bother hoping anymore. He's afraid to hope. Why don't you do something?! Don't you understand him?! Go! Quietly sit down next to him, and whisper in his ears the words, 'I understand.'"

Chapter 6

The Lie

True Self-worth

After just having heard a sermonette about how I had self-worth, I remember setting out to prove whether or not it was really true. I knew that God loved and valued me just as He loves and values His Son (John 3:16), but that was the value with which *God* viewed me. I also knew that my friends and family loved and valued me, but the perception of these people and God did not and does not create value in anything. To them, I was and am valuable, precious, and priceless, but I was not convinced. Did I really have a self-inherent value just because I existed, just because I was?

Having been taught to accept nothing as truth until I had first proved it to determine for myself whether or not it was true, I stepped outside on the porch and began using the deeper recesses of my brain in the quest for evidence to prove whether or not I really had any self-inherent value. My eyes scanned my surroundings as if searching for outward evidence. Finally, my vision rested upon a certain brick in the wall by the front door of my mother's house.

I did not ask myself the question, but rather the question came to me, "Does this brick have value?" I quickly concluded that the brick did have value, not much value perhaps, but value none the less. "Why does this brick have value?" I questioned. The best reason I could give as evidence that that one brick in my mother's house had value was nothing more than the fact that it was a brick. True, bricks are valued by man because they have a purpose, but even if bricks had no purpose, they would still hold value. Why, because it was a brick. It consisted of matter. Matter has value just because it is, regardless of whether or not others place value on it. Therefore, if the brick had self-inherent value just because it was a brick, then surely I had self-inherent value just because I was me.

The thought that I had value separate from the value with which others looked upon me was a shocking thought. "I have value?" I questioned. How could it be? Never before in all the past twenty-two years of my life had the thought ever entered my mind that I actually had a value separate from others. I knew I was *valued*, but I never thought that I had *value*. It was totally weird. I actually had self-worth.

Now, to take this even further, if I was never created, I could have no value. But since I was created, I have value. Therefore, my value came with my creation. The moment I was brought into existence, I had value. Therefore, since value is only present with an actual creation, it was my Creator then who gave me value in creating me. But exactly how much value did God give me? Since my value comes from Him, He is the only one who can rightfully say how much value I have. He is the only one who can rightfully say how much value anything has. Value comes with existence, and since He brought all things into existence, He has attached to all things a certain value. What man deems as most valuable, the Creator may deem as least. And so often what man deems as least valuable, the Creator deems as most.

How much value does the Creator place upon me? How much value does He place upon you? The Lord says, "Are not two sparrows sold for a farthing? and one of them shall not fall on the ground without your Father. But the very hairs of your head are all numbered. Fear ye not therefore, ye are of more value than many sparrows" (Matt. 10:29-31). The value placed upon the sparrows here was the value given them by men, two measly farthings. But farthings do not have life, and therefore, they cannot hold as much value as a sparrow. All the silver and gold in the world cannot ever equal the value of even one sparrow, much less many. That which has never had life can never come close to equaling the value of that which does, for it is only life that can beget life. Therefore, all the combined treasures of the universe cannot ever equal the value of even one human soul.

But exactly how much value has God *given* to man? Jesus said that man is more valuable than many sparrows. It was Jesus that gave them their value, and so He knows exactly how much each of them is worth. Both humanity and sparrows have life, and they were both given value upon their creation, but according to the Lord of life, the Giver of life, man has much greater value than many sparrows. How much value then does man have?

If you were to go to a silversmith and ask him the value of a certain piece of silver, upon examination he would tell you the price of the silver piece. The price of the silver is the indicator of its value. Relating this to us, how much did the Creator, the Giver of life, and the only one who can, therefore, rightfully determine our value, pay for us? What was our price? That's right. Even the very life of God!

"For God so loved the world, that he gave his only begotten Son, that whosoever believeth in him should not perish, but have everlasting life. For God sent not his Son into the world to condemn the world; but that the world through him might be saved" (John 3:16, 17).

Did you ever think that the value of your life compares with the value of God's life? Not because of your purpose and capabilities, but just because you are. Shocking thought isn't it? God didn't die for sparrows; He died for *you*, and therefore, your self-inherent value is more than that of sparrows and far more than that of mere silver or gold that has no life.

For those who believe that the gospel of Jesus Christ is true, it is theirs to realize the infinite value that they have. Not the value that others view them with but the value they actually *have*. But for those who don't believe, how shall they determine how much they are worth? In the evolutionist's mind, his self-inherit value cannot be any more than that of a frog.

> *I asked them, "What is the difference between you and a dollar?" "The dollar is worth more," they chuckled.*

Others may and do value him as more than a frog, *much more*, but his self-inherit value cannot be more than a frog, a sparrow, or anything else. And since evolution teaches that life came from no life, then that which has life cannot be valued as worth more than that which doesn't. Therefore, for the evolutionist, can he honestly view himself as having more value than a brick?

Things that are of high value are always guarded, simply because they are worth so much. Do you think it is any different with us? Even Satan admitted to the Lord concerning Job, "Hast not thou made an hedge about him, and about his house, and about all that he hath on every side?" (Job 1:10). And what about Elisha when he was surrounded by his enemies? Did not the Lord have "horses and chariots of fire round about Elisha" (2 Kings 6:17)? And what about the little children? Of them Jesus said, "Their angels do always behold the face of my Father which is in heaven" (Matt. 18:10).

Those who accept Christ, accept His protection. "Because thou hast made the LORD, which is my refuge, even the most High, thy habitation; *There shall no evil befall thee*, neither shall any plague come nigh thy dwelling. For he shall give his angels charge over thee,

94

to keep thee in all thy ways. They shall bear thee up in their hands, lest thou dash thy foot against a stone" (Ps. 91:9-12). "The angel of the LORD encampeth round about them that fear him, and delivereth them" (Ps. 34:7).

In life, the pain of rejection often proves overwhelming to us. The thought of not protecting ourselves against emotional pain is just plain horrifying. But in all this, we must not forget our self-worth, our value, our price. When we reach those low points in life and then finally hit rock bottom, if we look upon ourselves as worthless, or worse, *below zero*, we will treat ourselves as such. This rut is basically impossible to come out of, unless we see the value we really have. It is not enough to see that others value us we must see the value we have, that is ours, just because we are.

It is only natural for one to protect something that is of value. Therefore, if we see the value we have, it will only be natural for us to seek protection for ourselves. And since we learned that the best defense against rejection is no defense at all (see Matt. 5:39), although it may seem counterintuitive, we need to defend ourselves by not defending ourselves. And when we finally let go and stop trying to defend ourselves, we will then let the Lord take care of our defenses. He knows our value far better than we do because He gave it to us in both creation and redemption, and therefore, it is only natural for Him to defend it according to its worth—the worth of His own life!

But some are afraid to trust themselves with God. Why? Do you think He will hurt you? Do you think He will bring you emotional discomfort and pain? Is man more kind than God? Will the very Author of the principles brought to view in this book break every one of them for the express purpose of destroying those whom He has given so much value as to be compared with that of His own life? Oh no. He would never! Do you *know* the thoughts that God thinks toward you?

Now let's hit home base. What is the difference between you and a dollar?

If so, it is only because He told you. And if He didn't, it would be wrong for you to tell Him what they are. It is not for you to tell Him what He is thinking. Especially since you are the creation and He is the Creator. But since God wants you to know His thoughts and purposes toward you, He says, "*I know* the thoughts that I think toward you, saith the LORD, thoughts of peace, and not of evil, to give you an expected end" (Jer. 29:11).

The Lie—It's Birth and Life

The lie that we have no worth or value is planted in us very early on in our lives. I found out that I actually had value when I was about twenty-three years old, and it really took me for quite a spin. After the whole brick incidence, I asked someone what the difference was between them and a brick. They said they didn't know. Not getting the answer I was looking for, I asked them, "What is the difference between you and a dollar?"

"The dollar is worth more," they chuckled.

"Out of the abundance of the heart the mouth speaketh" (Matt. 12:34). Now let's hit home base. What is the difference between *you* and a dollar? Are you having a hard time admitting you are worth more? I wouldn't be surprised. Many people find it hard to accept the idea that they actually have great value. Yes, even more than a dollar—a lifeless piece of money! This is because the lie that was planted in their mind so long ago has been accepted by the mind as truth on a subconscious level for many years, and it is hard to give that lie up. And unless that lie is *directly* and *consciously challenged* by truth, we will perhaps never realize that we believe it.

But how is this lie that we have no worth or value planted in us and then accepted as truth by the mind on a subconscious level. The paths, or subconscious reasoning, for why we accept this lie can be numerous. But here are two fairly direct paths: 1) "That which is wanted has value. Since nobody wants me (a feeling), I must not have value." or 2) "That which is valuable, is protected. If I am suffering from emotional discomfort and pain, it must be because I am not being protected, and if I am not being protected, it must be because I have no worth or value." Yes, rejection is the reason that this lie is planted in our minds. And the experiences of life fertilize and water this lie until it becomes a monstrously enormous man-eating plant.

The reason it is so hard to give this lie up is because so much of our life, our thought patterns, our decisions, our actions, and our habits are based off of that lie. It is the lie that we are worth nothing that makes up so much of who we are today. The very way we think, *our very identity*, is based off of the lie that we've been accepting all of our lives and that has only been growing stronger and stronger as time and time again we suffer from the emotional pain that attacks our self-worth.

Rejection planted this lie very early on. It was nourished by continued feelings of rejection. This warped our belief system so that our thoughts more thoroughly revolved around this lie. And with our thoughts circling the lie, our actions and habits followed, all revolving around that lie. Thus, the feelings we feel, the thoughts we think, and the things we do, all making up who we are and determining the character that we possess, have been based on the one grand foundational lie that we have no worth and no value.

As an infant we suffered from rejection. Our developing minds concluded that we suffered this pain because we had no worth or value. Very early on *this painful lie became identified with the emotional pain that originated it.* During this most critical time of our lives, when our little minds were still developing, some of our very first subconscious conclusions were that we have no value. From this point onward, every time we suffered the pain of rejection, not only did we deal with that pain, *but because of its identity with the lie,* it triggered the pain of that lie. When suffering from rejection then, we are not only suffering from present pain but from the charged up pain of the past, and it is this triggered pain from the past that makes us seem so fragile and easily hurt.

This makes evident the fact that when we develop rejection habits to push people away, isolate ourselves, or whatever the habit is to protect us from rejection, those habits are formed, not so much to keep us from the pain of present rejection but rather to keep us from the pain of past rejection—the lie that you are *perfectly worthless.* Now that hurts! Thus it is proved that our life, our character, who we are, and our very identity, is based on and revolves around the lie.

> *Why would it matter? After all, it's just us. I mean honestly, who cares? It's not like we are anyone special.*

It is very important to note that when we suffer from present rejection, because the painful lie is triggered on a *subconscious level,* we do not look at the larger part of the pain as coming from the lie but rather as coming from the rejection at present. This is all wrong. When we make this false connection, it is not *the lie* that we determine is hurting us. Either we don't know where the pain is coming from (which is very frustrating) or we determine that the extreme pain we are experiencing is coming from *the people* who are presently rejecting us. But the overwhelming pain we feel is *not* coming from them. They did not give us that pain because *they are not the lie!* It is not their fault that we hurt so much. It is the *lie* that is hurting us, *not them*. We must get this point correct, or the temptation is to miserably hate them. And should we give in to that temptation, woe be to us all!

You—The Negative Particle

The people who subconsciously believe they have no worth always seem to look upon others as valuable. Though there be no difference between them, they will always view others as possessing value, but never themselves. Everyone around them is worth something, but they are not. In their subconscious mind, they are alone, isolated, and different, because they have no value. Everyone else in the room is a positive particle in their minds because they have value. But they are the odd ball in the group, *the negative particle*. If anything goes wrong, it must be their fault. They are the problem. And when the experiences of life teach them that everything bad that happens is their fault, it only drives them further into the pit of self-destruction.

When a child, because they didn't do it right, hears Daddy tell them they are "Good for nothing!" Because they broke it, Mommy scolds, "Why do you always break everything you touch?!" Because they didn't do better, their teacher sighs, "You disappointed me again." Because they made a mistake, their friends ask, "Why do you always mess things up?" Well, the answer is very simple; it's because "I'm the negative particle."

At whatever value we view ourselves as possessing, according to that value we will treat ourselves. So, when in our minds we don't have *any* value, when we are the negative particle, we see no point in taking care of ourselves. We may perhaps manifest the most tender care for others, but when it comes to us, it really doesn't matter. Why would it matter? After all, it's just us. I mean honestly, who cares? It's not like we are anyone special.

When we esteem ourselves as worthless, we don't care whether or not we eat junk that will destroy our mind and body. We don't care if we pollute our minds or drug up our blood stream. We may refrain from these things because of the value that others place on us and the love and care they have for us, but should all these people disappear, it doesn't matter what happens to us. There's no point in caring—no point in anything.

Ultimate Pain Relief

The emotional pain you suffer resulting from the lie can only hurt you because it lies to you. Truth will never harm nor imprison you. Oh no, "the truth shall make you free" (John 8:32). But lies can only cause you pain *as you believe them!* If you don't believe them, they cannot access your mind or affect your life. If I lied to you right now by telling you that your best friend had just died, my lie would only bring you pain if you believed it.

Only lies can attack your self-worth, because truth declares you very precious and valuable. Therefore, the emotional discomfort and pain *that attacks our self-worth* is powerless to *damage* us as long as we don't believe the lie that comes with it. If someone rejects us, especially if that someone is close to us, it can potentially attack our self-worth. When people reject us, we will feel the *pain* of *that* rejection, but it can only *damage* us as we believe the lie.

But lies can only cause you pain as you believe them! If you don't believe them, they cannot access your mind or affect your life.

It is not the pain of present rejection that is of greatest concern here. This pain will not kill us. It is the mental damage

100

caused by the lie that will end up taking our lives. The pain resulting from this damage is deadly because the wound is deadly. As long as you don't believe the lie that you have no worth and no value, you are safe from being damaged by it. Pain may come from present rejection, but it is not eternal, for the time will come when "God shall wipe away all tears from their eyes; and there shall be no more death, neither sorrow, nor crying, neither shall there be any more pain: for the former things are passed away" (Rev. 21:4).

How and Why It Kills

The reason rejection seems to hurt us so much is because it is a reconfirmation of the lie that we have no worth or value. This is the lie that hurts and damages us and that builds up pain inside of us, and when we are rejected by someone, it triggers the pain of that lie because it accesses the location of that lie where it is stored in the brain.

When sharing with someone a sad or painful experience that has happened in our lives, often we will feel the emotional pain of that experience again and may even begin to cry. Associated with that sad memory is a file charged full of emotional pain, and to feel that pain again, all we have to do

One's ability to help others, the value that others place on him, the dependence that others have on him, his accomplishments that he can show others, etc. become the only sense of worth that the individual has.

is access the memory attached to it. It works the same way with the pain that comes from the lie that we have no worth or value. If that lie is triggered, the pain comes back, and we feel it once again. Because we still believe the lie and because this lie is so often reinforced and repeated to us on a subconscious level every time we are rejected by another, we are always feeling the pain of that lie. Also resulting from the reinforcement of that lie through rejection is an increase of the pain associated with it. This pain will build up until it passes its boiling point, and the victim mentally explodes.

> *The body's immune system lays down its weapons and whatever comes, comes. There is no point in defending life, because life doesn't matter.*

In order for the brain to live, the mind must see that its life has value. Without this, it will begin to turn off. Because many people do not view themselves as having self-inherent value, the mind then places the value of its life on the only thing that it can—others. One's ability to help others, the value that others place on him, the dependence that others have on him, his accomplishments that he can show others. etc, become the only sense of worth that the individual has. Without this he has no purpose, no value, no reason to even bother existing. This is why our lives get tangled up so much in others that without them we figure we would just die. This is because we would. Without the value we have in them, and with no self-inherent value, our mind shuts down. This is why some people mysteriously die when someone really close to them passes away. All of their worth and value was tied up in them, and without them, their brain turns off. The body's immune system lays down its weapons and whatever comes, comes. There is no point in defending life, because life doesn't matter.

If our only sense of value is tied up in others, then when they reject us, it seriously affects the only bit of worth we have, most especially if that other person is close to us. In cases like this, the closer the relationship, the more our value is tied up in them. Should that person severely reject us, it will trigger most, if not *all* of the built-up pain of the lie that we have no worth or value. This pain is often very intense as it has had much time and ample opportunity to increase. Once triggered to a high enough level, the pain eventually can no longer be tolerated by the mind, and since it is thoroughly convinced that it has no worth or value, it begins to shut down.

Matters are made worse when, through the rejection process, we develop habits that push others away from us to keep us safe but in the end only hurt us more. When this happens the mind will realize that it is actually a danger and threat to others in whom it has its only sense of value. Since the mind's only sense of value is in what it can do for others, when it realizes that it is actually a danger to them, its value is deleted because now it can't do anything for others but destroy them. Terrible is the experience of those whose value is thus stripped from them, for they experience what it is like for the brain to actually commit suicide.

You're Worth It!

The only way to be safe from this lie that will lead to self-destruction is to understand our worth and value, which comes from our Creator. We can find our worth in God because He gave us our value upon creation and because He increased that value to an infinite level in giving His Son's life for us. It's not about how much we are worth to others and to God; it's about how much value we *actually have*. To just understand how much we are worth *to God* is not enough. It is a wonderful thing to contemplate, yes, but it is not enough. However, once we understand the self-inherent value we were *given* upon creation and which was *increased* to infinity upon the death of Jesus, it gives us a sense of value that will fill the void that many have had in their hearts since their very beginnings.

When remembering the true value we *actually have*, that *is ours*, that *belongs to us*, and that *cannot be separated from us*, remember that the lie, that we have no worth and no value, is just a lie. And as a lie, it is not real, and what it is trying to establish, does not exist. No, it is nothing more than a purple bunny, a red elephant, a green llama—*it's not there!* So go, be free from the lie, and thrive on the truth, because *you're worth it!*

"The grace of our Lord Jesus Christ be with you. Amen" (1 Thess. 5:28).

If anyone is interested in salvation because they
now realize just how much they are worth, then remember that
Salvation Isn't Free... It's Been Paid For!

And if anyone tells you that we are saved by works because these
somehow make us good enough, valuable enough,
worth enough to be saved, then you tell them that we are
Saved by Works... Christ's Works!

Both of these books
Salvation Isn't Free... It's Been Paid For!
and
Saved by Works... Christ's Works!
are written by James Prest and
published by TEACH Services, Inc.

We invite you to view the complete
selection of titles we publish at:

www.TEACHServices.com

or write or email us your praises,
reactions, or thoughts about this
or any other book we publish at:

TEACH Services, Inc.
P U B L I S H I N G

www.TEACHServices.com

P.O. Box 954
Ringgold, GA 30736

info@TEACHServices.com

TEACH Services, Inc., titles may be purchased in bulk for
educational, business, fund-raising, or sales promotional use. For
information, please e-mail
BulkSales@TEACHServices.com.

Finally, if you are interested in seeing
your own book in print, please contact us at

publishing@teachservices.com.

We would be happy to review your manuscript for free.

www.ingramcontent.com/pod-product-compliance
Lightning Source LLC
Chambersburg PA
CBHW060551100426
42742CB00013B/2519